SIDNEY BECHET: MY FATHER

MEMORIES FROM THE WORLD OF JAZZ

DANIEL-SIDNEY BECHET

DANIEL-SIDNEY BECHET

SIDNEY BECHET
my father

MEMORIES FROM THE WORLD OF JAZZ

Translated from the French by Ronda Lewis Draper

BOOKS
OF AFRICA

Included with the book a free CD of Bechet's music, "Homage" played by Daniel's own Jazz Quintet with a contribution from the internationally known African Jazz Musician and Saxophonist, Manu Dibango...

Publisher:
Books of Africa Limited
16 Overhill Road
East Dulwich, London
SE22 0PH
United Kingdom

Web site: www.booksofafrica.com
Emails: admin@booksofafrica.com
sales@booksofafrica.com

Copyright : © Books of Africa 2014

ISBN : 978-0-9926863-4-5

A CIP catalogue record for this book is available from the British Library.

First published in France by A vos pages ; original title: Sidney Bechet, Mon Père

© French text : Daniel-Sidney Bechet and Fabrice Zammarchi
© Photos : Daniel-Sidney Bechet and R. R.
Printed and bound in India by Imprint Digital

I have the utmost admiration for the instinctual science of jazz saxophonists.
It sometimes happens that the saxophonist becomes intoxicated by the rhythm
And begins a monologue in the void
As some drunkards talk to themselves
Repeating endlessly.
Such a thing never happens to Bechet.
He never babbles; he articulates.
And his words are always passionate
And powerful. They come from the heart.

Your poet, Jean Cocteau
Saint-Jean-Cap-Ferrat, 19 August 1959

Sidney Bechet - the British Connection

by Howard Rye

Sidney Bechet was the first acknowledged jazz great to set foot in Great Britain. As he is also reckoned second only to Louis Armstrong in the artistic hierarchy of his generation of New Orleans jazz musicians his arrival gave a very auspicious boost to the start of the jazz age in Britain.

He arrived on 14 June 1919 as a member of the Southern Syncopated Orchestra, which should not be conceived of as a jazz band. It was a large orchestra, said to have a repertoire of about five hundred songs, and played a mixture of jazz, ragtime, spirituals, Victorian and Edwardian popular music, light-classical music, instrumental novelties, and anything else which was, or could be played as, a distinctively African American style. The orchestra's success, which enabled versions of it to tour in Britain and Europe until 1922, must have owed much to its combination of familiar forms from the ragtime and earlier eras with up to the minute new sounds. More than one commentator observed continuity with the musical *In Dahomey*, starring Bert Williams and George Walker, which the orchestra's leader Will Marion Cook had presented in London in 1903.

Bechet stood at the other extreme. Grenadan trumpeter Arthur Briggs, later a jazz musician of some moment himself, expressed the view to Bechet's biographer John Chilton that Sidney was the only real improviser in the orchestra's line-up. "We had various players who could embellish melodies and play variations in the symphonic style, and we also had musicians who could re-interpret a melody with ragtime phrasing, but Bechet could and did play pure jazz and blues." This was equally obvious to musically informed contemporaries, exemplified by a deservedly revered critique by the Swiss conductor Ernest Ansermet which is quoted in this work. The *Cambridge Magazine* noted "Mr. Sydney Bechet, who extemporizes a clarinette solo about ten o'clock, and compels admiration, so true is his ear and so rhythmical and vital his conception." A century later, it would be hard to improve on this critique.

At the end of 1919, Benny Peyton, who was one of the orchestra's drummers, formed a small jazz band to play at the Embassy Club in Old Bond Street. Sidney Bechet was a member of this band, which later became known as The Jazz Kings during long residencies at the Hammersmith Palais de Danse and Rector's Club in Tottenham Court Road. They were playing at Rector's in September 1922 when Bechet had the spot of bother with the law which led to his deportation. At the time of his arrest he was living at 27 Southampton Street, Fitzroy Square, now 27 Conway Street, following a name change in the late 1930s. It is very much hoped that a "blue plaque" recording Bechet's association with this address can soon be in place.

Bechet did not play in Britain again until 13 November 1949, when he made a surprise guest appearance with Humphrey Lyttelton's band at the Winter Garden Theatre, in London. This appearance earned its promoter a conviction under the Aliens Order which cost him a £100 fine, since at the time the Musicians Union barred American musicians from working in Britain and their stance was supported by the Ministry of Labour. Earlier in the day he had recorded six titles with Lyttelton's band for the Melodisc label.

It may cause surprise that no action was taken against Bechet himself or even that he was let in at all. His Home Office file reveals the surprising fact that his deportation order was reviewed in 1931, when one "C.P.H." wrote on his file "Name to be deleted from Suspect Index. Offence trivial, a doubtful case, assaulting a prostitute, but his character seems to have been good. Deportation Order revoked." It has been speculated that this development might be connected with Maxwell Knight, better known as the prototype of the "M" of Ian Fleming's James Bond novels. In private life, Knight was a jazz enthusiast and amateur clarinettist. Guess who he took lessons from back when Rector's was the happening place to be for the musical avant garde.

Bechet visited Britain again in September 1951, when he played at a private party, somewhat nervously it seems. It was not until 1956, when an exchange agreement was finally worked out between the British and American musicians' unions, that he was able to play in public again. A two-week nationwide tour, which visited Glasgow and Belfast, culminated in a concert at the Royal Festival Hall in London on 16 September. He came back as a star to general acclaim.

This was not quite the end of the British connection. On 15 May 1958, he appeared on the BBC's current popular music vehicle, *Six-Five Special*. His appearance was transmitted live from the Caveau de la Huchette in Paris with the co-operation of French broadcasters. Sidney was interviewed by compere Pete Murray and played *St. Louis Blues* accompanied by Maxim Saury's band. A year later he was gone.

Howard Rye is an independent scholar of African-American music. He is co-author of the current edition of 'Blues & Gospel Records 1890-1943', (Oxford, 1997), and is a member of the editorial team of the research journal 'Names & Numbers'. His series 'Visiting Firemen' in 'Storyville' magazine documented in detail the activities of African-American musicians visiting the British Isles. In 2009/10 he guest-edited 'Black Music Research Journal' issues devoted to the Southern Syncopated Orchestra. He is co-author of 'Black Europe', two volumes and 44 CDs published in 2013 documenting the sounds and images of the African diaspora in Europe up to the mid-1920s.

INTRODUCTION

On May 14th, 1959, exactly 50 years ago, my father, Sidney Bechet, breathed his last note. Ravaged by lung cancer at the age of 62, his rapid death had a terrible impact, devastating his fans, his fellow musicians and especially his family. Especially myself. It's always too soon when you lose a loved one. This sounds trite, I know; it is nevertheless true.

I often regret all those moments I was not able to spend with him, all those secrets I would have loved to share with him, to ask him about his past, his life, his music, his doubts, his fears, all those things that make up a man and mould a child, because five years is too short a time in which to know one's father. The time spent together at this young age creates impressions. It doesn't really permit an exchange of ideas or real communication. I sometimes have the impression that he belongs more to a collective memory than to me. But it is also thanks to this and to numerous testimonies that I have been able to get to know him better.

It is not always easy sifting through the stories and the emotions he provoked, especially the expressed hostility and the coarse, insensitive comments. Luckily I have a good dose of humour and an appreciation of the ridiculous; also and an emotional distance which enables me to grasp and deal with certain situations and events with equanimity.

I want to share with you, through my father, his life and the world of jazz, all that I am, what has moulded me, and my heavy ethnic and musical heritage - this bewitching, disturbing, generous, implacable world in perpetual evolution.

I will try to tell you about his origins, rich and distant, about the same blood that runs in my veins His story has been presented in a number of books and biographies, but never in an intimate, personal and sincere way. I hope this book, like a musical score in black and white, will persuade you to follow me in the footsteps of my father!

Daniel-Sidney Bechet

Omar

A while back I read the autobiography that our father left us, *Treat it Gentle*, later translated into French with the title, *Musique c'est ma vie* (Music is My Life), and it left a deep impression on me. I remembered everything in it, and after thinking about it for many years, I came to realize that I was the last link in a great chain, a long relationship which had its origins deep within time. In fact, it went back to a time before jazz had been invented. It is a very long story with its roots tied deeply to those of the Black people, a people of Africa who were deported from the African continent to the Americas. This is one of the worst tragedies known to humanity, commonly known as slavery. Although my father had not lived it himself, he was greatly marked by this inhuman ordeal which his community went through, and he discussed its effects when he wrote about his journey in *Treat it Gentle*.

My father's grandfather was named Omar. He was a slave who also possessed a great musical gift. He knew how to dance,

Josephine Michel (Sidney's mother) and two cousins.

sing, play the drums, and he also had the innate spirit of a leader. Sunday was the day of rest for the slaves who gathered at Congo Square in New Orleans. My great grandfather was the one who gave the signal for the festivities with his drums; he was the one who beat the rhythm for the songs, the dances and other rituals. The slaves blindly obeyed all of these commands.

Omar made his own drums and other percussion instruments out of the skins of pigs and horses. Although a slave, he held a special status because his master gave him the freedom to practice his art - and this was well before emancipation! It should be understood that this ancestral communication via the tomtoms and drums went back to their distant Africa, and for these men reduced to slavery the drums sounded like a promise of freedom. This is how music was born, with its tumultuous mixture of rhythms, its muted growing rumblings echoing without end. As my father would say, it was in this primitive musical organization that the very first form of jazz was to be revealed: ragtime. Congo Square was also the place where slaves destined to work on the plantations were bought and sold.

One night Omar had a nightmare. He dreamt that he lost the use of his right arm that was somehow cut off at the elbow. From that moment on, he began, more or less consciously, to use his left arm in all activities, in case the dream turned out to be a premonition. His friends fell under his spell when they heard him hit his drums. They would circle around him rhythmically treading and stamping on the ground together. It was like a magnet and everybody was attracted to these rituals and ceremonies, even theWhites, especially the plantation managers who had to constantly watch and control their slaves.

It was during one of these trances that Omar's destiny hit him. He saw a young, beautiful slave, Marie, and in an instant he fell madly in love with her. Unfortunately, her jealous master kept a vigilant eye on her, wanting her for himself. Insanely furious to find that the young girl preferred Omar to him, he did everything in his power to separate them. Despite this, the two lovers finally met and the master found them lying side by side. In an explosion of anger the master grabbed the young slave by her arm and opened fire on Omar. The bullet lodged in his right arm and my great grandfather could do only one thing- flee as fast and far as possible. Despite his wound, Omar managed to escape his trackers by going deep into the bayou, but he was now a fugitive slave. He began looking for the slave hideout in order to find his strength again. But danger remained omnipresent because there were wanted posters of him in all the neighbouring towns and plantations promising a rich reward to whoever returned a runaway slave. Omar's wound was so serious that they had to amputate his right arm for lack of any first aid. And so his nightmare became true. During this time, the master had regained control of himself and began crying, "Rape! One of my girls has been raped!" The man's lie seemed to be true and people believed him. People gathered around him and believed it to be the literal truth. A Black slave had raped a White woman! A posse was quickly formed, ready for lynching! After days and nights of being hunted, Omar was betrayed by one of his own: a slave who, attracted by the reward offered for his capture, didn't hesitate to kill him while he slept to bring him back to the plantation. However, my father added: "And the guy who killed my grandfather, the guy who pretended to be his friend so that he could safely assassinate him, he didn't even ask for his reward. He stayed there, rooted to the place, without a word. They told him to go away, but he didn't budge. He seemed not to want to leave. They had to threaten him before he reluctantly left " Following this tragedy, my father concluded his story: "My grandfather was really a chief, a leader of men. For music it was a fearsome beginning."

My Father

Whether real or imagined, the story of my father's grandfather's tragic ending became the essential source of his creativity. This ancestor with whom he identified represented an ideal for him to follow, giving him direction in which to grow. When he played, my father put himself into some sort of trance during which he took into account everything that Omar must have suffered in an effort to overcome it and then to transcend it through music. This explains, in my opinion, the extreme motivation that animated his music and the force of conviction that animated him. It was complex but, I believe, it brought him to a fuller expression. Whenever someone asked him about his music, my father would always say, "I play what I live!" In his autobiography he concludes: "This young woman, Marie, had a child. Given my grandfather's tragic ending, she knew neither what last name nor what first name to give him. She still lived in the master's big house when the child came into the world. The master and his wife advised her to give the child their own family name: Bechet. And so he had a name... she had her son and it was as if she kept something of Omar close to her. And so she called him Omar. Omar Bechet: that was my father.[3]" I never met my grandfather. I learned through papa's book that after emancipation he became an artisan shoemaker on the Avenue de l'Esplanade in New Orleans. He was himself very interested and gifted in music and he learned to play the horn. But he was an especially excellent dancer, and it seems that is how he first seduced my grandmother. She confided to my father, "the first time I saw your father, your future father... he was wearing such pretty shoes. They were beautiful, and he danced so well... I could only see those elegant shoes and the marvellous way he danced in them... and I fell immediately in love with him!" Omar, my father's father married Josephine Michel and she gave him seven children. Sidney, my father, born on May 14, 1897, was the youngest in the family.

SIDNEY BECHET

*W*e cannot forget the greatest of them: Bechet ! *The greatest of all creatures, Bechet, the symbol of jazz! I heard him before he left Washington. He always played the same way. From that time to just before his death. I remember hearing him play "I'm Coming, Virginia" in 1921… It was the most extraordinary thing I had heard in my life. I had never heard anything like it before. It took my breath away. He played the clarinet when he was in New Orleans, but after he took up the soprano saxophone, he didn't want to play anything else. And yet he was an excellent clarinettist. His clarinet had a fantastic, robust sound to it, one that they don't make anymore. The guys in New Orleans really learned something while they were learning the Albert system. I think of Bechet as the starting base. Everything he played came from the soul, from inside. It was extremely difficult to find his equal. He could prepare an improvisation in his head while someone played, then he'd play one or two choruses, or more, that blew every-thing away. He played with us in 1926 when I had an orchestra in New England. Johnny Hodges learned a lot from him, especially the soprano sax.* (Duke Ellington)[1]

---

1. Stanley Dance, interview, 1962.

It is extremely difficult, impossible even, to explain the genesis of jazz in America. It is a musical phenomenon that slowly appeared, and essentially in New Orleans, and it is linked to a socio-cultural context. In this southern American port scarred by slavery and with much ethnic mixing, an amazing musical melting pot flourished. You could hear African drums, the blues, Negro spirituals in the churches of the Black community, military marches from the Civil War, French and Spanish quadrilles, Irish dances, Italian opera and music imported from Europe in the White community. Between these two apparently irreconcilable cultures an intermediary caste developed, that of the Creoles, people of mixed race from various cultural and linguistic origins: French, Spanish and African. They often had Spanish names: Tio, Manetta, Perez; or French names: Robichaux, Picou, Bigard, Baquet and... of course, Bechet. All these early men of jazz were born from the effect of French and Spanish colonization on black slaves imported from Africa. Consequently, certain Creoles, based on their percentage of African blood, found themselves in a veritable musical crossfire Blacks, remaining close to their African roots, infused a certain energy into the mix through the use of drums, ecstasy-inspired polyrhythms, and improvisation. The Creoles brought musical education, technical ability and the repertoire. Skillful instrumentalists and good readers, they also frequented the opera and were often music teachers.

My father was somewhere between the two. As a child he had watched and listened to it all. His position in a Creole family and his attraction to music had logically prepared him for his meeting with the clarinet, a noble instrument among Creoles.

Sidney child, elder 3 years.

He began studying it at a very early age, albeit informally. Leonard Bechet, my father's elder brother, played the trombone and tried his hand at the clarinet. My father would secretly borrow it from him and practised with his mother's agreement: "My brother Sidney, when he was small, would hide his school books and go play the flute. I never knew that he played, you know what I mean? At that time I had a clarinet and I had put it up on high in the closet with the idea of giving it to him one day. I asked my mother if Sidney was using it. She told me he was. So I asked him to show me what he could play. It was pretty good. From that moment on Sidney took off and I was never able to catch up with him. Sometimes, when I watched him, I thought his mouth had the same shape as the mouthpiece on the clarinet. It was all so easy for Sidney, you know what I mean?[2]"

It was within the family circle that my father experienced an important musical event. His mother surprised her son, Leonard, on his birthday by inviting an orchestra- and not just any orchestra! It was the trumpet player Freddie Keppard's band, one of the most popular in New Orleans. That evening, the clarinettist George Baquet was supposed to play, but as he was late, the orchestra had to start without him. Seeing this, my father took his clarinet and, sitting at the back, he began to

---

2. Alan Lomax : *Sidney Bechet*, Jean-Roland Hippenmeyer, Genève, Tribune Éditions, 1980, p. 35.

play with the orchestra, first softly and then increasingly loud. The orchestra first thought that Baquet had arrived, but when they realized that was not the case, they stopped playing and looked around to see where the sound was coming from. That was when they discovered a little ten-year-old kid sunk in a big armchair. This was one of my father's first exploits. When Baquet arrived, he was very nice and let him play beside him in the band all night long. After this incident, George Baquet and then other Creole teachers lined up to instruct him, but they had to bow to my father's rebellious character. He said, "I studied for awhile with George Baquet but, to be honest, he didn't seem to have anything new to teach me. What I mean by that is Baquet was a helluva musician, a wonderfully good player. But he wasn't really what you could call a ragtime musician. What he played wasn't really jazz though because he stayed really faithful to the melody, like it was written. And he always played so seriously. He was much more classical than 'Big Eye' Louis Nelson. When Baquet played, there weren't any of those gyrating sounds or the wide vibrato that was a part of ragtime music. This was how musicians' personal sensitivity interpreted the music... All that moaning and groaning along with a certain jubilation. There was none of that in the way that George Baquet played. I don't know if he couldn't do it; all I know is that he didn't. After awhile I stopped going over to his place. I started taking lessons with 'Big Eye' Louis Nelson, but that didn't last long[3],"

Having been marked by those haunting stories of slavery, my father wanted to play the blues, and that was not the type of music that Creoles valued. He wanted to create a music that related directly to what all men of colour had suffered in the

3. Sidney Bechet, *LaMusique c'est ma vie*, Paris, La Table Ronde, 1977, pp. 117-118.

United States. As soon as he could, he composed an ambitious piece entitled *Negro Rhapsody, the Voices of the Slaves.* That was in the 1920s. Unlike the musicians of his generation who tried more often than not to ignore reality by pushing it deep into their subconscious, my father gave it voice: "All the music that I play comes from everything that happened when my grandfather was alive. It's a bit like water- flowing silently, perfidiously, pouring out and engulfing submerged rocks, slowly, patiently wearing them down until they disappear. All the pains, the torments and cries which later gave rise to spirituals were not yet in any order. It was later that ragtime incorporated them, gave them form and brought this message to those who needed it, to those who could understand, and which helped the whole world to understand its , profound importance[4]."

Every Sunday my father would listen to the Negro spirituals sung in his neighbourhood church, St. Augustine's, where he was baptized in 1897. He gave us his vision: "In the spirituals, people clapped their hands. That's how they kept the rhythm. With the blues they swayed… the rhythm was always there. And both the spirituals and the blues were a prayer. In one we called to God and in the other we called to the humanity in man…. Spirituals have within them the potential to create a state of ecstasy, letting the person transcend pain. It's like a man who closes his eyes and so can see a light within himself… Spirituals are a means of seeing this light. It's a faraway music, a means of escape, but this opens a path for you. Blues are like tears, like an awful feeling of solitude. There are so many memories inside, so many horrible things to remember, an overwhelming feeling of frustration. But the two genres are based on the same rhythm…

---

4. *Ibid.,* p. 72.

It's as if they're coming and going at the same time.[5]"

Right from the start my father refused to learn to read music, letting people know that the music he heard in his head had nothing to do with the little black notes printed on paper. Instead he began to play by ear the tunes he remembered and improvised around it the rest of the time. This was the new concept of variations on a theme. He never had to tie himself down to fastidious textbook exercises to develop his technique. Through personal dogged hard work he quickly became one of the great improvising clarinettists in the city.

My father was not the only musician gifted with imagination. An older clarinettist who fast became his role model caught his admiration: 'Big Eye' Louis Nelson could make his instrument sing like no other and he didn't use sheet music either. Leonard Bechet, his older brother, was worried about the influence that Nelson had on his brother: "In our family, we were very well brought up. We stayed at home and didn't run around the streets. We didn't want to ruin our parents' good name by hanging out with riff-raff. We were worried a lot when Sidney spent the night out playing. Guys like Bunk Johnson drank a lot and we didn't like Sidney being with guys like 'Big Eye' Louis Nelson and Jimmie Noone[6]." Tuned into everything happening around him, my father was attracted to the raw, savage expression of what was being played in the Black community. Without giving up on a more traditional clarinet style, he was blown away by the powerful percussions and the extraordinary rhythmic pulsations during parades and by the intensity of their blues. Their music was a source of joy and it made people wild to dance. That is why my father chose

5. *Ibid.*, p. 265.

6. *Ibid.*, p. 3.

to bring together the two styles. At that moment he became a part of history when he became the clarinettist who connected these two cultures. He was not the only one, of course, to bring about this osmosis; it was the work of an entire community. But he was the symbol of it. The fire which he brought to his clarinet stemmed from the percussive quality of his notes as he beat out the tempo, something which created an inebriating vibrato and a blaze of sound unknown until then. My father became one of the greats of this revolutionary American music which jazz became in the early 20th century. He was one of the four founding fathers, the others being King Oliver, Jelly Roll Morton and Louis Armstrong – and that statement is as true as the fact that the Eiffel Tower stands tall on its four pillars in Paris.

Early Triumphs

Papa was precocious. At the age of 13 he became a professional musician. Music represented everything for him. It was his most basic necessity, and he never saw himself doing anything else in life. After playing in every part of New Orleans, his birthplace, and gaining the maximum experience possible, he felt the need to stretch his legs, so he started going on tours. First Chicago and then New York, he knew that was where the future looked the most promising. In 1919 my father was far from rolling in dough in the streets of New York. However he was meeting important people, like the singer Noble Sissle and the orchestra leader Jim Europe who was touring with a military band. Noble Sissle talked about his first meeting with my father: "One evening when I was at Charlie Lett's Café on State Street, someone pointed out to me a small thick-set guy

Sidney and Freddie Keppard, Chicago, 1918.

seated at the bar and suggested I listen to him play the clarinet. The man added he was sure to be picked up by Jim Europe for his orchestra if he ever heard him play. I went over and asked him if he would play something for us. He said okay. I didn't see any instrument lying around so I asked him, 'can I go get your clarinet for you?' to which he gave a small mischievous smile and answered, 'no thank you, I have it right here.' Then to my surprise I saw him put his hand in his pocket and fish out part of a clarinet, then from another pocket, this time in his overcoat, another piece, and then he pulled out the mouthpiece from still another pocket. He started to piece these oddments together under my very eyes, and taking some chewing gum, he glued the pieces together while he stretched elastic bands of differing lengths to activate the keys. Then he adjusted a reed tip that looked more like wrapping paper than anything else, it was so thin and worn. But when he told the big band leader to play the piece he had indicated to him, I can tell you I had never heard such a beautiful sound coming out from even the most beautiful clarinet in the world. Sidney played a strange 'blues', with a sound that was both honey-like and powerful. It gave me shivers all up and down my spine. The next day, I came back with Jim Europe who, when he heard him, got all flushed and wanted to hire him on the spot. I reminded him that our tour was over in Boston the following week and that he had to take a much-needed break since it would be the first one since the US declaration of war. That didn't stop him from his negotiations with Bechet, making an appointment in New York to start the season at the Hotel Shelborne at Long Beach[7]." Things did not work out but they give an idea of the seductive power of my father's talent, particularly on big band leaders.

Characteristic Blues

Europe attracted him, too, and quite logically my father accepted an offer to go and play in London in the summer of 1919. This first trip was important for what followed. My father, an accomplished soloist, became part of a quintet under the leadership of Will Marin Cook. He played *Characteristic Blues*, his personal favourite, before King George V and Queen Mary at the Philharmonic Hall in London. In the audience there was also the renowned classical conductor Ernest Ansermet. Astounded by what he was hearing, Ansermet went to see my father afterwards. This is what my father said about the encounter: "Every night a man came to hear me play. He would sit behind the orchestra and he loved to hear us talk. It was Monsieur Ernest Ansermet. One day he asked me if I sang into my instrument in the same tone that I was playing. I told him, 'I don't sing, I play like that.' And since he thought this seemed rather novel, he wrote an article in a newspaper[8]." Then "Several times he came asking me questions about my playing

7. *Jazz Hot*, n° 241, 1968, translation by Ch. Delaunay
8. Raymond Mouly, *Sidney Bechet, notre ami*, Paris, La Table Ronde, 1959.

and my instrument, what I was doing, was I singing into the instrument to make it sound like that. We talked for a long time about music. Ernest Ansermet was a classical conductor but he was greatly interested in our music. There was no end to the questions he asked and I don't think he missed one performance. He was there every night[9]." The London Press gave my father the title "King of the Licorice Stick"! But I prefer to remember what Ansermet wrote about him: "In the Southern Syncopated Orchestra there is an extraordinary clarinet virtuoso who, it seems, is the first of his race to have composed on the clarinet blues of an accomplished form. I heard two pieces which he had worked out at length and then played for his fellow musicians so they could accompany him. Extremely different one from the other, they are both equally admirable for their rich inventiveness, their strength of tone, the boldness of their novelty and unexpectedness. They already give the idea of a style, and their form is striking, abrupt, impetuous, with a well-defined and implacable ending comparable to that in Bach's Brandenburg Concerto No. 2. I want to say the name of this musical genius, because I will not forget him: it is Sidney Bechet. When one has so often looked back at one of those figures to whom we owe the birth of our art, those men of the 17th and 18th centuries, for example, who with their dance tunes created expressive works of art, thus opening the way for Haydn and Mozart who were not the initiators but were the first to make a success of this music. There is something so moving in the meeting with this stout boy, completely black with white teeth and a high, narrow forehead. He is so happy that we love what he is doing, but he is unable to say anything about his art, except that he is following his "own way". And

9. Sidney Bechet, *op. cit.*, p. 170.

when one thinks about this "own way", it is possible that this main road will be where crowds will flock tomorrow[10]."

With hindsight, it seems that this lucid and enthusiastic article represents the first jazz critique ever written. We need to put ourselves into the context of 1919 Europe and realize that my father had brought about something revolutionary: African-American music. There are a few comments to make about this article. First, it gives an idea of the technical mastery shown by my father. Ansermet spoke of an extraordinary clarinet virtuoso, and coming from him this is no small thing. His daily exposure to clarinet virtuosos in the symphony orchestra made him an expert. The most important detail, in my opinion, was the unique way my father had of making his instrument sound. This expressionist style full of growls and hoots, with an enormous vibrato and livened by a big influx of rhythm, had fascinated Ansermet. There is one last thing important to consider as proof that my father had his place as one of the pioneers of jazz: we are in 1919 and if we believe Ansermet's judgment, he had reached maturity. His style was of the moment, not from yesterday.

Historically speaking, the first jazz album had been recorded in 1917 by the Original Dixieland Jazz Band, a White band in New Orleans. They recorded *Tiger Rag* and *Livery Stable Blues*. My father had explained: "At the time a few White musicians had started imitating our style as well as they could. They played pieces that were actually our own. But it had nothing in common with our music - there was nothing of us in it. I don't really care what people think, but it is extremely difficult for a man who is not Black to play a melody that comes from

10. *La Revue Romande*, 1 October 1919.

the depths of the Black experience. It's a matter of sensitivity. All those White musicians went to play in New York. The studios recorded them. The public became infatuated with this music and the record companies gave people copy cats, the nearest to the real thing. We can't really call this New Orleans music because it ain't. And since this music needed a name, it was baptized Dixieland. And that is how they came up with the name of the Original Dixieland Jazz Band with Larry Shields[11]." That happened in 1917 and listening to these records one can easily understand what my father was trying to say. The band's clarinettist, Larry Shields, was far from possessing the maturity my father had at this time. It is impossible to imagine that he could have caught Ansermet's undivided attention for more than a second. It was not until 1923 that the American recording studios brought to the world, for the first time, proof of the exceptional musical talent of Sidney Bechet. My father didn't record his *Characteristic Blues* until 1937, and when we listen to it we have a vague idea of what Ansermet heard twenty years before.

The Song of Songs

In his critique Ernest Ansermet spoke about two types of blues, but the trumpeter Arthur Briggs who played in the same group explains to us: "Bechet often expressed himself in a series of pieces, first playing blues, then a popular tune in which he could show off his vertiginous technique[12]" . This long stay in London was important to my father's career because it was there that he familiarized himself with the soprano saxophone. He was strolling with Arthur Briggs down a London street when he saw

11. Sidney Bechet, *op. cit.*, p. 155.
12. *Jazz Hot*, n° 3, December 1945.

a shiny new one in a shop window. Briggs reported that he asked if he could try it and he played *Whispering* without the slightest mistake despite playing this instrument for the first time. It was love at first note. After he bought it, he immediately began playing it in the London clubs. All of the qualities that he had developed on the clarinet he applied to the soprano saxophone and he became the uncontested king of this instrument. He created his own personal way of using and understanding the soprano sax. His first success in London was called *The Song of Songs*. Seldom used, this instrument was ideal for interpreting the melodies he loved with its soft caressing sound and its incomparable fullness of expression. He was also attracted by the operatic music he heard in New Orleans and he often cited his two favourite lyrical singers, the tenors Enrico Caruso and Richard Tauber. Their highly dramatic delivery expressed in an intense vibrato had a considerable influence on my father's style. My father managed to express himself like no other soprano sax player,, with an incredible attack, enormous power and suppleness, to the point that this difficult instrument between his fingers and lips became a perfect means of expression. This is how he began playing it regularly alongside the clarinet. This new instrument would slowly be instrumental to his future glory.

Despite Ernest Ansermet's enthusiastic testimony, my father did not break through at that moment and he continued to work in relative anonymity. This promising period had an unfortunate ending that was much less glorious. One night, my father had an argument with a girl in a London bar, and things went badly. When the police arrived they hauled him away. After the pretence of a trial where he was never given the chance to defend himself, he was put in prison for two weeks and put on a ship back to New

Portraits from police records, London 1922

York. My father experienced the racial prejudices of the time in a country where a foreigner was barely tolerated. The situation was quite ironic for a man that, not long before, had been applauded by King George V, whose face was on British coins. And so, while on the boat to New York my father suddenly had a strong desire to take all the English coins in his pocket and throw them into the sea. This gesture gave him a sense of relief similar to what you feel when you wake up from a bad dream.

Wild Cat Blues

Papa was a prolific composer all through his life. The first musical theme he composed in America, back in the 1920s, was called *Ghost of the Blues*. He never had the opportunity to record this piece before he moved to France, though. It wasn't until he was in Paris, in 1952, that he recorded it for posterity by Vogue, with Claude Luter's orchestra. Black musicians had a hard time building a career in America, but despite this, my father recorded his first albums in 1923 while he was playing at Clarence Williams' club, the Blue Five. These historic recordings show he was ten years ahead of his time compared to his musical contemporaries. It was enough to hear him play *Wild Cat Blues* on his soprano sax to know that he was already an accomplished virtuoso. It was a piece composed by Fats Waller for the piano. My father took it and made it one of the first greatsaxophone solos in the history of jazz. It corresponded so well with his wild cat temperament and it made him a legend among the musicians who were stillin New Orleans. But it was also on the rhythmic level that his supremacy could be measured. His overflowing imagination pushed him to play more and more complex phrases without losing the beat. This involved a certain amount of risk-taking and his competitors on the instrument could only bow down before his talent. This is what is called having natural rhythm. At this time these first jazz records were called "Race Records,", and we can only acknowledge the discrimination inherent in this term.

The field of opportunityfor a freelance musician was enormous at this time. In 1924 there were 238 dance halls licensed in New York, without counting the hundreds of more or less illegal nightclubs which employed musicians. My father would go from one establishment to the next all night long with his soprano sax, playing a piece in each, always leaving to thunderous applause. One musician who watched him do this, fascinated by his behaviour, was Johnny Hodges: "He would play just long enough to make 40 or 50 bucks then fly off to the next club. He was really extraordinary[13]" That year papa

13. John Chilton, *Sidney Bechet, TheWizard of Jazz*, London, McMillan Press LTD, 1987, p. 67.

was solicited by Duke Ellington to join the Washingtonians. In the drummer Sonny Greer's words, "Sidney Bechet came one evening and pulled out his soprano saxophone. Right on the spot, Bubber, Charlie Irvis and he started jamming. It was great. So we hired him and he played with the Washingtonians on the clarinet and on the soprano sax. He fitted in like a glove... one night, all the bands met up at the Palais Royal to play for some charity gala... as soon as we started playing, the whole room was electrified. The third piece we played was one of those improvised ones, played in our style, and Bechet, Bubber and Charlie moved forward. Bechet took a table napkin which he held in his mouth and let it hang in such a way as to hide his fingers while he played his soprano sax. He blew everybody away... Bechet always played *Dear Old Southland* on stage and he had a lot of influence on Johnny Hodges. He liked Johnny, and Johnny studied his style. But Bechet was always a drifter who wanted to see what was happening elsewhere[14]." Duke Ellington did not want to be outdone by them but "Bubber Miley and Bechet had the habit of competing musically every night, and that gave a huge boost to the orchestra. They would take five or six themes at a time and while one played, the other would leave the stage to have a drink. They were like two picturesque gladiators[15]."

In July 1925 my father decided to open his own nightclub in New York thanks to a big sum of money from royalties from his compositions and from the recording sessions with Clarence Williams. It was a dream of independence. He hired Johnny Hodges, who had become his student, to play in his

14. Stanley Dance, *Duke Ellington par lui-même et ses musiciens*, Paris, Filipacchi, 1976, pp. 73-74.

15. Duke Ellington, *Music is My Mistress*, pp. 73-74.

band. When Hodges was interviewed in the 1950s, he said, "the biggest influence on me was Sidney Bechet. I had already had the chance of playing with him before he came to work with Duke Ellington. Around 1923 I heard him in Boston when he came with the Jimmy Cooper revue. My sister knew him and spoke a lot about him. After hearing him, I never missed an occasion to hear him play whenever he came around. I finally got myself a soprano sax and one day asked him to blow into it. Then he played with me. Much later, every time I went to New York I would spend a few evenings in his club on 7th Avenue. He would also have me listen to his latest and say, 'listen closely because the old man won't always be around!' The reason I was so influenced by him is that he seemed to be so different from all the other musicians of the time. A lot of saxophonists were trying to play like Benny Carter, Coleman Hawkins or Jimmy Dorsey. Me, I wanted to be like Bechet. Of course Louis Armstrong also impressed me with the albums he made with Clarence Williams or with the Hot Five. But above all, what counted for me was Sidney Bechet[16]."

My father opened a cabaret called Club Basha. That's how the musicians pronounced his name, and it quickly became the hot spot for the underworld. My father remembered having seen Al Capone himself walk in. He had the habit of entering the place and laying his revolver on the piano as, a way of marking his territory, and when he did the place would become highly charged. The smallest incident could have turned into a blood bath since everybody was armed. This was the time of prohibition. Stories of prostitution, rigged bets and racketeering caused my father to declare his club insolvent. The situation became more and more dangerous for him and

16. Raymond Mouly, *op. cit.*, pp. 49-50.

I suspect that he accepted an engagement in Europe because it was becoming urgent for him to put some distance between himself and the New York scene.

"The Talking Saxophone"

My father benefitted from a new opportunity which brought him back into the spotlight in 1926 when he participated in the *Revue Nègre* in Paris at the Théâtre des Champs-Elysées. Exoticism was all the craze in Paris and the Who Who's of the painters and writers of the Parisian art world such as Blaise Cendrars, Fernand Léger, Robert Desnos and Francis Picabia were there. The star of the show was Josephine Baker. She was an overnight success thanks to the lascivious way she swayed her hips, and she was quickly hired by the Folies-Bergères.

My father played in the orchestra and accompanied her on stage, and he, too, made a big impression with his solos on the

Josephine Baker and Sidney at the Théâtre des Champs Elysées. Paris 1925.

Sidney in Russia. 1926.

clarinet and soprano sax. In an interview the theatre director, André Daven, described his entrance on stage: "The curtain rose and a fantastic skyscraper painted by Paul Colin and on the huge empty stage behind a small multico-loured street seller's cart Sidney Bechet appeared, blowing a melody of extraordinary sweetness, overwhelming with its melancholy. The purest of notes emerged harmoniously. It was an enchanting moment. Within thirty seconds murmuring from the audience died down and on the last heart-rending note the hall broke out in thunderous applause[17]." But there were others there, intellectual reactionaries such as René Bizet who wrote: "Nobody had better try to tell us after this show that Americans are modest. These Blacks are masters of the grotesque caricature. There is no finesse- or very little- in their irony. Their actions are so undisciplined that you cannot see the difference between their frolics and St. Vitus's dance[18]."

After several weeks in Paris, the *Revue Nègre* went on tour but my father didn't want to stick around. The wind of freedom had always been an important element guiding his career. He wanted to see the country and he began to take long trips all over Europe, going as far as Russia. He would always remember with nostalgia the people of that country who welcomed him like he had never been welcomed before. On

17. Joséphine Baker et Jo Bouillon, *Joséphine*, Paris, Robert Laffont, 1976, p. 67.
18. *Ibid.*, p. 69.

Sidney playing baritone saxophone at the Gross Frankfurt *in Frankfurt, Germany. 1927.*

the concert hall posters he was billed as "The Talking Saxophone" and the Russian people appreciated his message. The romanticism of the Russian soul resonated with his lyricism, and in the decades to follow, he continued to have a burning desire to return one day.

During his meanderings all over Europe, Paris remained his favourite home base. In the summer of 1928 he was the soloist for Noble Sissle's orchestra at the Ambassadors Club on the Champs-Elysées. Sissle remembered an unforgettable evening: "The Ambassadors was at that time considered to be the most exclusive interna-  tional meeting place. Sidney had chosen the soprano-sax because of its softer sound and the effect on the public. His biggest success was when he was playing for me, and the best proof of his genius was when we played for an evening gala for 750 guests at The Ambassadors at the height

Portrait. 1926.

Portrait. 1926.

of the horse-racing season in Paris. The "Who's Who" of the racing world were crowded together and the hubbub literally drowned out the sound of the orchestra. Bechet asked me to let him play a solo on the soprano: *The Song of Songs*. I told him that nobody would listen, but he just smiled. I thought he wouldn't have any effect because the public wasn't paying us the slightest attention. They were more occupied eating, and the sound of the cutlery on the plates was creating an enormous din. So I let him play, and Sidney stepped forward from the band and faced the room. He went to the front of the stage and threw his head back as he raised his saxophone to his lips. He didn't want to be backed by the piano. You could hardly hear him being introduced, but right from that first, interminable note he played, silence fell. 750 forks and knives stopped as if by enchantment, the waiters froze and the entire public turned as one towards him. You could only hear

Noble Sissle's band at the Ambassadeurs, *Sidney on the right. Paris. 1928*

Bechet. At the end of his solo, I witnessed the most wonderful ovation that the most blasé audience in the world could give a musician. This "Big Week" was devoted to Sidney Bechet on the Champs-Elysées.[19]"

This testimony enables us to understand the impact my father had. He wanted to be heard at all costs and it was also a challenge for him constantly to evaluate the power he exercised over the crowds. He had a lot of friends in Paris. He hung out at boxing rings and often met colourful personalities such as Eugene Bullard. This man had lots of contacts and knew how to solve problems when they arose.

While he was living at Pigalle in Paris with his companion, Elisabeth, at the end of 1928, my father was mixed up in a

19. *Jazz Hot*, May 1968, translation by Ch. Delaunay and quoted in *Sidney Bechet*, Jean-Roland Hippenmeyer, p. 82.

serious situation which cost him dearly. Elisabeth told me later that she never knew how everything ended. It seems that at six in the morning, papa burst into the apartment where they were living, grabbed his revolver and went right back out. "I learned from the concierge and the newspapers that two musicians, one of whom was Sidney, had fired on each other right on Rue Fontaine," explained Elisabeth. One of the newspapers, the *Intransigeant*, related the incident in the following words: "Fighting Niggers at Montmartre. Three passers-by are wounded." This episode is without a doubt one of the most dramatic my father went through and he was very open about it in his autobiography. He said himself that he could be a swine, and the moment he opened fire on his aggressors, he was in a horribly swine-like mood. But he didn't apologize even though he recognized that he had behaved badly. According to Elisabeth, there was a girl involved, but my father told us

it was about racism. The man who instigated the dispute was a piano player from Chicago by the name of Glover Compton, an inveterate liar who constantly boasted and who hated my

Sidney at the
Florence Cabaret,
Paris. 1928.

father. Because he didn't have the guts to tell papa to his face what he thought of him, he chose as an agent provocateur a young banjo player named Mike McKendrick, an easily influenced boy who was also from Chicago. With bits of gossip and later with insults, McKendrick needled my father until he lost his temper and things went sour. At 8am the two musicians found themselves at the door of the tobacco shop on Rue Fontaine and the conversation turned poisonous. My father was hot-tempered and was quickly provoked. Bragging that he was from Chicago in the north of the United States, McKendrick felt he had the right to remind my father how Blacks were treated in the South, especially in New Orleans, mentioning horrible attacks from harassment to lynching. Talking about this was the worst thing he could have done. That's when gunshots were fired. Things happened very quickly. McKendrick and my father were only slightly wounded. But Glover Compton who had come

Sammy Richardson, X, Sidney Bechet, Frank "Big Boy" Goodie. at Pigalle, Paris 1928.

to the rescue heard the shots had a bullet in his knee without doubt from my father's gun. Two other people were wounded by ricocheting bullets, one of them critically. After the police arrested them, they found themselves at the police station on Rue de La Rochefoucauld, still in their tuxedos, their shirt fronts spotted with blood. It went to court andboth the banjo player and my father got sixteen months in prison, despite their lawyers' efforts. While my father served his time in prison at Fresnes, Glover Compton tried to put him on trial a second time so he would stew behind bars even longer. He had been off work for two months which put him in a difficult financial situation and he now walked with a stiff leg. He wanted revenge but my father made him understand that if he continued, he had better watch out for his second leg. This story had heavy consequences and fed gossip about the violent temper my father could sometimes show, which was a fact. He never looked for a fight, but he knew very well how to defend himself. I remember a funny detail that wraps up this story. In the sixties the television director Jean-Christophe Averty was in the United States doing research on jazz. In Chicago he found Mike McKendrick and decided to question hm. When he reminded him about the Pigalle incident with Sidney Bechet and the resulting incarceration, McKendrick didn't say anything. He immediately got up and left Averty. He kept a stubborn grudge towards my father as well as towards France although it had made him a celebrity after the incident. When my father got out of prison after eleven months, he was not allowed to stay on French soil. Now considered an undesirable, he returned in 1931to the USA which he didnot leave for 18 years.

Maple Leaf Rag

My father had a hard time making it in America. Segregation was a major reason for this and it affected everything. It influenced the whole music scene. Duke Ellington's orchestra, made up entirely of Black musicians, played at the Cotton Club for an exclusively White public. This was a very smart place yet Blacks were not admitted because they were too poor and especially because of this segregation and discrimination. My father did a tour with this fabulous big band and renewed his contract with Johnny Hodges and his boss Duke Ellington. He played as a soloist and one of his special pieces was *The Sheik of Araby* in which he played a "special chorus" that Hodges would take up later.

Then he directed his sextet to play at the Apollo in New York and made a series of fantastic albums, among them *Maple Leaf Rag*, a pure jewel. That being said, I notice with some curiosity that he used the word ragtimeto designate the music that he was playing although at that very moment it was only part of his selection. *Maple Leaf Rag* is the best example of the evolution from this piano ragtime to the jumping syncope which papa took to play it in three time. This monument of dynamism and swing assured Bechet's role in the natural evolution of jazz. The economic crisis of 1929 wiped out show business to the point that my father had to give up music in 1933. With his friend, the trumpeter Tommy Ladnier who shined shoes, he opened a laundry business in the middle of Harlem on Saint Nicholas Avenue. They had to make a living, but he didn't become bitter. After a day of work, he would invite his musician friends, also out of work, and they'd have a jam session until the wee hours of the morning.

One night Noble Sissle showed up in his store and wanted to put him back in the saddle, so to speak, because he had a star soloist position that had become vacant. When my father returned to the profession, America was in the middle of the "swing era", when jazz was played by big White orchestras in the big hotels for dancing. Two good clarinettists took the top billing: Benny Goodman and Artie Shaw. They had big careers and made lots of money. The White musicians were all inspired by Black musicians. The connection is not hard to prove. Benny Goodman owed part of his style from Jimmy Noone, a colleague of my dad from New Orleans; it was the same thing for the trumpeter Harry James, another big name from the swing era, who was inspired by Louis Armstrong. These were White musicians who profited financially from the commercial development of this music.

My father spent long periods of time in the thirties in Noble Sissle's big band with whom he had already played. It was not the biggest band but it had quality. That is where he met the singer Lena Horne. Most of the time he played wherever he was the most useful in the band which explains why Sissle used him as a bass saxophonist in the rhythm section which was unworthy of his talent. In reality, Sissle was aware of his great talent as a soloist and, whenever he could, he put him at the front of the band and had him play the clarinet and the soprano sax to attract the public.

My father had two "battle horses." One was the *Polka Dot Stomp*, a super swing piece of his own composition, and *Dear Old Southland*, a hymn to the South to which he remained attached all his life. You have to listen to this piece. It's a veritable concerto for soprano saxophone and big band jazz, a matchless masterpiece with an intro that will take your breath away and a coda that reaches the mountaintops. But all of this is not without clashes and resentments because the entire saxophone section, jealous of their status, would throw him the proverbial banana skin to trip him up by refusing to follow him. But my father knew how to handle these situations. The same thing happened to him when he played with Duke Ellington in 1924 and the brass section of the band tripped him up for similar reasons.

He also had friends in Sissle's orchestra, one of whom was the trumpeter Demas Dean who talked about the type of showmanship musicians had to do: "While we played with Sissle at the Apollo Theater in 1936, Lena Horne would be sitting at a small table singing *Dinner For One Please, James* while Bechet, in the role of James, the maitre d', would serve her something to drink. It was absolutely sensational. Then Sidney would literally propel the show forward when he would take up his soprano and start playing *Dear Old Southland*. He was the best and he'll never be forgotten[20]."

Chant in the Night

After leaving Sissle in 1938, my father started recording a great deal because the American jazz world was experiencing a return to the beginnings which was called the "New Orleans Revival." The RCA Victor Company had him sign an exclusive contract and he found himself regularly in the recording studio with the great jazzmen of his generation. The numerous sessions organized from 1937 to 1941 show us the extent of his skill and are considered by the critics as the best of his entire

20. Roland Hippenmeyer, *Le « Cas » Bechet*, anniversary leaflet, Genève, 1989, p. 9.

career. This is where he recorded his biggest clarinet solos. We have to mention *Blackstick* which superbly describes the instrument in question; *Blues in Thirds* with the pianist Earl Hines; the complete masterpiece *Egyptian Fantasy*; *One O'Clock Jump* with the young Kenny Clark; *Perdido Street Blues* with the great Armstrong; *Twelfth Street Rag* with its devilish pace, and many more. But already at this time my father preferred by far the soprano saxophone and many masterpieces were recorded with this instrument. For example there is *Chant in the Night* with its twilight melody; *Indian Summer* with its luminous serenity; the poignant *Blues in the Air*; and the exhilarating *Lime house Blues* and *Stompy Jones*. To appreciate his stupefying mastery of the soprano sax, I recommend *I Know That You Know*, played at supersonic speed when he aligns one acrobatic phrase after the next with negligent ease. This was the time when papa recorded a *Blues for You, Johnny*, in honour of his New Orleans colleague, the clarinetist Johnny Dodds who had just died.

Dodds was the archetypal New Orleans style clarinettist, and he once mentioned my dad in an interview: "Bechet is truly great, and nobody has ever played like him. Damn it he was he good!" and he grunted and shook his head to underline what he had just said. I asked him if Bechet knew how to read and Johnny got all excited and pointed at a pile of magazines; "Bechet couldn't read one word of anything in there, not one word, not even the title!" Then he picked up a big volume on the table and said to me: "If this was in F minor, Bechet wouldn't know it. But have him listen to something just once and he could play for you like nobody had ever played it before!" Johnny smiled and it was touching to see the pleasure he got from talking about Sidney[21]." This witty comment unfortunately perpetuates the belief that my father was a semi-illiterate musician. All the people who worked for him would tell you the contrary: my father could read, write and arrange music. He was a complete musician. I do admit that he was not a fast reader, however. Maxim Saury told me he would not have been able to hold his own in an arrangement written for a saxophone section. That wasn't his specialty. But he could read enough to be able to decipher a simple score. He also wrote music, but slowly. There are scores written in his hand but he preferred using a tape recorder to save what he had and his ideas for themes. Also, as far as harmony was concerned, he didn't fear anybody because he had been playing the piano since he was a child. No one knew exactly when he had learned to play. As soon as there was a piano in the room, my father would rush over to it because he was constantly tuned into his music.

Throughout his life he composed about a hundred pieces and two ballet scores without ever having set foot in a music school! He was allergic to teachers of all sorts. People confuse self-learning and musical illiteracy. For his recording sessions, Luter would say that my father dictated the sequence of chords to the pianist and would give each musician their note to play for the background. It's enough to listen to the album *Blues in the Cave* recorded later for Vogue to understand this. When it came to harmony Papa was a very advanced musician, very modern in fact! He was ten years ahead of his contemporaries. For example, he was one of the first to use the minor sixth chords, the augmented fifths, the diminished sevenths, and the ninth and thirteenth chords. He was capable of rolling off

21. *Music and Rhythm*, November 1940.

for you all these chords in all the tones on his soprano sax at lightning speed. His agent Charles Delaunay, who supervised the recording sessions, gave his opinion on this: "He was strict and determined about what he had decided to record. He could enter the studio and record ten numbers in three hours, simply because he knew exactly what he wanted to do before he got there. If one of the musicians had a doubt, Sidney would play what he wanted him to do on the soprano, and he would then sit down at the piano and play the harmonic progression without skipping a beat. He was truly an extraordinary musician[22]."

In 1941 my father was also a pioneer in the art of overdubbing in America. *The Sheik of Araby* was recorded by him with six instruments: soprano and tenor saxophones, clarinet, piano, bass and drums. What is remarkable apart from the excellent execution is the depth of his knowledge of what each instrument had to play in a small improvising band. And one last detail: he played the « special chorus » which he taught to Johnny Hodges- on the tenor sax!

"School of Music"

Unfortunately, when the United States entered the war, it put a brake on his rising fame. Papa was not recruited because he was already close to fifty years old. In 1943, with no gig in sight, he even had to work a short time as a longshoreman on a construction site. He wasn't afraid of doing what had to be done to survive.

When world peace returned, it opened a new period of music in the USA. Having matured during the war years in the Black cabarets, a new style of jazz was born: bebop appeared on the

---

22. John Chilton, *op. cit.*, p. 251.

Portrait. New York. 1944.

Leonard Bechet. New Orleans. 1944.

New York scene in reaction to swing which had made a fortune for White jazzmen. Charlie Parker and Dizzy Gillespie were brilliant protagonists of it. A foreigner to this revolution, my father, nevertheless, continued to create his own musical groove. After the war, there were profound changes in the music profession. All over the world there was a new wave of the New Orleans Revival, particularly in Europe. In New York, my father started playing with a whole new generation of White musicians a bit younger than himself. The Chicagoans would all call upon the veteran he had become. The record company Blue Note called on him often and the excellent records which he made at this time were a foretaste of his future in Europe.

This was also the time when my father opened a music school in his home in Brooklyn. Tired from the constant touring, he had long had the idea of passing on to others the style of music he had been practicing all his life. Right in the middle of the bebop explosion, he had a line of students, all White and adepts at the New Orleans style. He wrote on a sign outside his house: "Sidney Bechet School of Music." Sincemusic was always evolving while still firmly anchored in tradition, he believed he had a lot to offer.

One student in particular was more assiduous than the others and would later be the best. This was the clarinetist Bob Wilber.

Portrait with "his" clarinet 1945.

time. I had met him one or two years earlier… his parents asked me to take care of him. Bobbie knew how to read music very well but he didn't know how to play an instrument. He couldn't play anything. He wanted to play but didn't know how to go about it; so that's what I taught him, that and how to produce different sounds, and even sounds with a big vibrato, a kind of grunting noise. His parents told me, 'you're working that poor boy too hard.' But he came back…, when that young kid first came to find me, he thought that the clarinet was easy to play. He would tell me, 'but I can't play all that without catching my breath.' So I told him to drink a little sherry to buck him up. He was a bit anaemic then. And his parents told me, 'you see! He shouldn't be drinking that. You make him work too hard.' I answered, 'I have to buck him up or he'll never have enough puff.' He continued to come and see me and in less than two years Bobbie became very good on his instrument[23]." Bob Wilber became so good that

23. Sidney Bechet, *op. cit.*, p. 234.

he went and played duos on the clarinet and the soprano sax at the end of the evening at Jimmy Ryan's, the jazz club where papa was a regular player. Bob said: "He had the impression that the next generation wasn't interested any longer in an older style of music, that everybody was listening to Charlie Parker and Dizzy Gillespie, and that they didn't want to know anything about his style of music. I believe he also had the impression that his time had come and gone. He never imagined that he could become the celebrity that he would be in France. I think he was convinced that he would spend the rest of his existence in a sort of semi-retirement, and that, perhaps, his school would bring him some income. He even thought he would only be

Bill and Ruth Reinhardt with Sidney. Chicago. 1949.

able to play occasionally…. Everything that happened to him later in France showed that he hadn't the least idea of what could happen to him in his lifetime[24]." This school didn't earn much for my father, but he had the satisfaction of seeing the musicians of the younger generation were not as indifferent as one might have thought to the style of music he had always promoted. At the end of the forties, having acquired the status

24. Jean-Roland Hippenmeyer, *op. cit.*, p. 192.

Sidney in New York. 1948.

of jazz veteran, which gave him respect, he worked regularly, sharing time between New York, Chicago and Philadelphia. But all this was no comparison to the turn his career was about to take.

Summertime

Liberated from the yoke of World War II, Europe experienced a prodigious craving for jazz. It was the music of youth. France, in particular, under the guidance of Charles Delaunay and Eddie Barclay, was attracted to music from across the Atlantic. Louis Armstrong came to play at the first post-war festival which took place in Nice. The next year, in May 1949, the second festival took place in Paris in the prestigious *Salle Pleyel*. Delaunay did the place up when he had the idea of giving top billing to Sidney Bechet and Charlie Parker, two of the biggest saxophone stars. Parker represented the peak of American modernity, whereas my father incarnated the purest of "trad" since he was older than Louis Armstrong. Can you believe what happened next? In this same Paris which had driven him away twenty years before, my father, by the magic of his talent, was a smash hit for an entire week in the immense Salle Pleyel. There was no guarantee that this would happen. Charlie Parker came with his bebop quintet with Max Roach at the drums. Miles Davis, not yet a big star, also came with his own band with another great drummer, Kenny Clarke. My father came alone. Charles Delaunay, who hired him, assured him that he would find two French bands that could accompany him.

The two bands in question, and which followed the New Orleans style, were those of Pierre Braslavsky and Claude Luter's *Lorientais*. They had been playing since the end of the war in the jazz clubs which had flourished in Saint-Germain-des-Prés. Made up of keen young musicians, these two bands were still amateurs and, by an incredible roll of the dice, found themselves playing with a master of the style they had chosen.

Photograph of bearer

This passport, properly visaed, is valid for travel in all countries unless otherwise restricted.

This passport, unless limited to a shorter period, is valid for two years from its date of issue and may be renewed upon payment of a fee of $5 but the final date of expiration shall not be more than four years from the original date of issue.

American citizens traveling in disturbed areas of the world are requested to keep in touch with the nearest American diplomatic or consular officers.

American citizens making their homes or residing for a prolonged period abroad should register at the nearest American consulate.

SEE PAGES 6, 7, AND 8 FOR RENEWAL, EXTENSIONS, AMENDMENTS, LIMITATIONS, AND RESTRICTIONS.

Sidney's passport.

The miracle of this story is that, though competing with highly experienced bands, my father still won by a head supported by groups that were still amateur. It was also the magic of the most direct, approachable style around. The night of the first concert, Bechet played the first half and Parker was to play the second half after the interval, but after the audience's delirious enthusiasm for my father, the "Bird" as Parker was nicknamed, had a hard time getting the audience to listen. They started chanting all together, "Be-chet! Be-chet!" Happy with the effect he had on the audience, papa felt bad for his

Stamps in Sidney's passport .

younger competitor, and he confided back stage, "the poor boy must be allowed to express himself!" The adjective 'poor' was an allusion to Parker's drug addiction. In the documents recorded during these concerts, you can hear my father in the final jam session playing frenzied riffs behind Charlie Parker! This shows that jazz is a single unique music, no matter what style is being played.

Papa had a huge impact on the public, as can be heard in the interpretation of *Summertime* with Pierre Braslavsky's orchestra where he holds the auditorium spellbound. Frank

Sidney Bechet, Bob Wilber, Ricky Wilber, "'Big Chief" Russell Moore, "Hot Lips" Page. New York. May, 1949.

Ray Sonin, Charlie Parker, Sidney Bechet. Paris. May, 1949.

Oran "Hot Lips" Page, Sidney Bechet. New York. May, 1949.

Ténot was present at these festival evenings and he wrote: "This is why when he pointed his soprano saxophone at the two thousand listeners at the Pleyel in May 1949 and blew the way he knew how, *Summertime* was infused with a half a century of racially mixed music, rhythm, passion, humanity and pride. Even before hearing the waves of acclamation, Sidney understood that in Paris, this was not about business, it was about love. Here he could be himself, be recognised and be indispensable. It was the Promised Land.[25]" The numerous audiences which crowded the Pleyel were eclectic. Just as Ernest Ansermet , a top classical performer, accompanied by his musicians, thirty years before had not missed one performance given by my father, now it was the violinist Alfred Loewenguth, famous for his own quartet. When the latter was interviewed, he was asked, "what did you like best about the festival?" He answered, "Sidney Bechet by far ..." and he added, "I love everything about Bechet! Everything! His phrasing, his power, his seemingly unlimited inspiration, the way he develops a theme. There's everything with Bechet: that miraculous intuition that you only find in exceptional people, the blowing, the grandeur, the pathos and the serenity of great musicians, joy too... and then there is this incomparable sound, this way of making every note and every silence live, this way of vibrating, this technique that you can feel but it never becomes showy. This dynamism, this force of nature... you can tell he is crazy about his art, and that, for this man, music has a vital function. How wonderful it would be if all musicians were like him.[26]"

Among all the ballads my father interpreted, *Summertime*

25. Fabrice Zammarchi, *Sidney Bechet, Passport to Paradise*, Paris, Filipacchi, 1989, p. 13.
26. Alfred Loewenguth, *Jazz News*, October 1949.

Sidney Bechet,
Claude Luter.
Paris. 1950.

had a special place. He made it a hit every time he played the melody on stage because the audience vibrated as one with him and accompanied him on these flights played in a minor key which he delivered like a great orator. He played at least twenty versions, some more majestic than others, throughout his recording career. The one he gave in Geneva on May 14, 1949 is without a doubt, though, the best of all. They are all emblematic of his way of recycling a song that was not his own and making it a personal work of art. This reminds me of when he tried to explain to us the difference between White and Black expression, and he shared his belief (perhaps a bit too slanted) about this song from the American operetta by George Gershwin, *Porgy and Bess:* "That isn't real jazz. There is certainly musical feeling in it. It's a nice bit of revue, and it's enjoyable, but that's as close as it gets. There are one or two pretty songs in it. *Summertime* is one of them. It's pretty and you can get the closest to the feeling of Black music in this song. But listen to it carefully. You can find the same feeling in it as in the *Saint Louis Blues*. So it's not authentic. I have great respect for Gershwin. He's a fine composer. All his music has great beauty and feeling. It tells a whole story by itself. But it's not Black American music. His music doesn't say what a man of colour would say, play or feel.[27]"

Les Oignons

My father fell head over heels in love with Paris and he was the right man at the right time in the right place. The fling then became an idyllic relationship while my father slowly decided to stay in France for the rest of his career, making his home port the *Club Vieux Colombier*. This place was situated in the middle of Saint-Germain-des-Prés, attached to the theatre of the same name. Charles Delaunay had foresight when he offered my father an exclusive contract to record for Vogue Records in the autumn of 1949. *Les Oignons* dates from this time. It was Sidney Bechet's first hit in France. Thanks to the broadcasting of this album on the radio, my father slowly became the popular artist he then continued to be with the French public.

He began touring the country with the clarinetist Claude Luter and his orchestra. According to his agent Charles Delaunay: "The tour in France went well, and at this time, we began to record our albums, one of which during the first sessions was *Les Oignons*, which began to be talked about all over France where jazz was catching on. This tour worked so well that Luter had only one dream: to have Sidney come and play with him all the time. So he planned to have him come to the *Vieux Colombier*...."

27. Sidney Bechet, *op. cit.*, p. 257.

At the Vieux Colombier. *Paris. 1954.*

The club at Juan-les-Pins, for example, was much bigger than the one in Paris, and this would bring in more money and help him to pay Sidney a better salary. That being said, Sidney Bechet on the "business level" was one of the rare ones, for an American and a musician in particular, to never ask prohibitive rates. His rates were always reasonable. He made as much as Luter's orchestra, and I believe that the going rate at the time was something between 150,000 or 200,000 francs (£150-£200). The orchestra got half and Bechet the other half. Sidney, on the international level, was worth a whole lot and everyone who hired him was pretty sure they would make money. The result was that after two or three years, the news obviously got around to organizers of Sunday dances, Saturday bashes and charity shows! Bechet managed about 300 concerts a year- it was incredible![28]" And the constant work at the Club *Vieux Colombier* helped the band to make progress and they were ready to play the moment

28. Jean-Roland Hippenmeyer, *op. cit.,* p. 181.

With Claude Luter and Pierre Braslavsky, at the Vieux Colombier. *Paris. 1949.*

Sidney stamped his foot three times to start a number. Thanks to the boss of the *Vieux Colombier*, Annet Badel, a very smart businessman, the town of Antibes Juan-les-Pins had a second club opened with the same name where my father played the summer season.

Through the years he became a popular local star. At that time he was at the zenith of his career because all the conditions needed were present to make good music and for him to become a celebrity. As Jean-Christophe Averty once confided in me, the popular music that young people were listening to was of exceptional quality, something which was far from the case later on. After *Les Oignons*, the piece that had a big success was *Moulin à Café* (coffee grinder). It was a virtuoso piece as well as being papa's last clarinet solo. It was his last stand, so to speak, on this instrument. He had been alternating between the

Claude Luter, Guy Longnon and Christian Vienot. Juan-les-Pins. 1951.

Claude Luter's band playing at Sidney's marriage. Juan-les-Pins. 1951.

Marriage cortège. Juan-les-Pins. 1951.

Elisabeth and
marriage at J
1951.

Between pages 63 and 66

...He had been alternating between the clarinet and the soprano saxophone as far back as 1920 when he lived in London, but he preferred the soprano more and more through the years. He saw that his solos had more of an impact on the public with this instrument, especially when he played a ballad. The soprano showed itself to be ideal as well in its ability to react to his dominating temperament....

Sidney's wedding, The
wedding cortège.

Mistinguett
marriage. Ju
1951.

"Sugar" Ray Robinson, Sidney Bechet, Prince Ali Khan. Juan-les-Pins. 1951.

to his dominating temperament thanks to the volume and power he could get out of it. At the end of the forties in America, he began to set aside the clarinet because it no longer satisfied him. He still used the Albert system which had fallen out of favour and been replaced by the Boehm system. The old Czechoslovakian clarinet he had been using no longer satisfied him, and when he came to France, Selmer's made him a brand new one for Albert system. Despite this, he put it away definitively in 1950, after having recorded *Moulin à Café* with Luter. I have to add that using two difficult solo instruments gave him twice the work. Once again, my father brought the house down everywhere he went the moment he started blowing his soprano saxophone. Especially in France he did not have the same result with the clarinet; this was due to the tonal qualities of the instrument. The decision didn't take long to make. All of his big successes in his French period were recorded with the soprano, except for *Moulin à Café*.

To alternate with the lively numbers in the New Orleans repertoire, papa composed an impressive quantity of blues. We have for example *Society Blues* and *Bechet's Creole Blues*, and his investment in this music never faltered with the change of continent, from the United States to Europe. He literally educated the French public about the blues, although at first it had been strictly Black music. He gave it a universal character and the public was won over. Bechet and Luter also toured Switzerland and Belgium. Jean de Trazégnies, a Belgian columnist, analyzed the reason for their wonderful musical understanding, in concert as well as on record. Under the title, "Sidney Bechet and Claude Luter, Two coryphaei of Joy", he wrote:

"Sidney Bechet, the Creole with the big heart, has exchanged the New York jungle for the gardens of the Ile-de-France. He must certainly feel more comfortable in the shade of the chestnut trees in the Luxembourg garden than surrounded by the concrete blocks of 7th Avenue. He has truly adopted Paris as his home and Luter as his support band. We have Claude to thank for that, because many French musicians who tried the New Orleans style, and he is among the famous soloists. If

Sidney and Elisabeth's wedding ceremony at Juan-les-Pins. August, 1951.

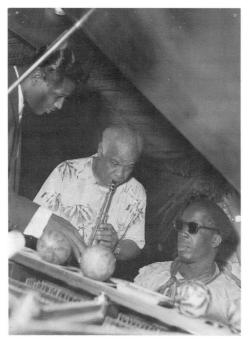

Sugar Ray Robinson,
Sidney Bechet at the Vieux
Colombier. *Juan-les-Pins.*
1951

Bechet preferred Claude Luter, he has his reasons, and they are not naïve ones. I have already written that Luter, even if he has not invented anything new, has the immense merit of playing well, a music that is right up his street.... Compare the first Blue Stars with the wonderful series at Vogue, and you will see how deeply the musicians captured this polyphonic vitality which was the charm of the old New Orleans records. You will see how much they evolved in interpretation, helped and galvanized, of course, by the serene and vigorous presence of Bechet... On the records that concern us, the role of the band is central. It is wonderful that a group of young people still full of idealism could play with one of their idols who was part of the pioneering era. The talent of Claude Luter and his fellow-musicians is not to be found in innovation or in brilliant virtuosity. If truth be told, these guys have something better than talent. They have faith in something beautiful: a belief in the youth of the heart, something our jaded time no longer knows. The best reward for their virtue is without a doubt this coming together and collaboration between these young White boys touched with grace and this sixty year old Black man whose youth seems eternal[29]*".*

29. *Hot Club Magazine*, February 1951.

Petite Fleur

In 1951 two new compositions written by my father were produced and they reflected this period of the fifties without being reminiscent of his New Orleans roots. One was *En Attendant le Jour* (Waiting for the Day), a romantic slow number that he would play at the *Vieux Colombier* late in the night, and the other was *Promenade aux Champs-Elysées* (A Stroll on the Champs-Elysées), a piece of light-hearted swing which evoked the deep feelings that tied him to Paris. This piece was taken up by the singer Virginia Vee (formerly of the Peters Sisters) who included it in her repertoire. There is a trace of this song in French variety performances, as can be heard in Joe Dassin's famous *Aux Champs-Elysées* which is far from being a copy and yet cleverly manages to catch the spirit of Bechet's song. I think the presence of Pierre Gossez who plays the soprano sax in this song pays homage to the

Sidney and Claude Luter's band in Morocco. 1952.

Moustache, Sidney, Elisabeth, Yank, Roland Bianchini, X, Pierre Dervaux, Gib. Grigny. 1952.

French award for musical recordings, and Bechet began to have sales that rivalled those of popular artists such as Edith Piaf, Charles Trenet and Jacques Hélian. Over the years, papa recorded several versions of *Petite Fleur*. The first one was done in studio with a slow-rock tempo for dancing and accompanied by a short piano solo. That was the version on on the jukebox in the decades that followed.

Lil Armstrong, Sidney Bechet, Beryl Briden. Paris. 1952.

But it was in concert that my father gave the fullest expression to this piece, because the presence of the public urged him onto a greater intensity of expression. The most deeply felt versions which he played with a two year gap were played at Salle Pleyel and at the Olympia with Claude Luter. In the first one, its honey-sweet sound and its lyrical flight of fancy completely transcended the melody, and in the second he made a veritable concerto for the virtuoso saxophone with it. The popularity of this number was at first confined to France. Curiously enough though, the version of *Petite Fleur* played by the British clarinettist Monty Sunshine and his quartet, recorded in 1956 is the one that became a hit. From that moment on record companies had their performers record this song and *Petite Fleur* became an international success. For papa, this was the first time in his life that his music was a success in the American market. As a sign of appreciation, he sent an autographed picture to the British clarinettist with the following dedication: "To Monty who made *Petite Fleur* in the Sunshine."

The same year as *Petite Fleur*, papa composed three other pieces which also had a huge success: *Dans les rues d'Antibes* (In the Streets of Antibes), *Le Marchand de Poissons* (the

Claude Luter and Sidney Bechet at the Vieux Colombier. *Paris. 1954.*

Fishmonger), and *Si tu vois ma mère* (If You See My Mother). This last one is a superb sentimental ballad dedicated, as you can tell by the title, to my mother. *Le Marchand de Poissons* was inspired by the old market place in Antibes which he frequented a great deal. My father wanted to give a nod to the many trader she chatted with whose stalls were stocked with fish from all over, something which reminded him of his home town and its port. *Dans les rues d'Antibes*, with its lively marching beat, became almost a local anthem because Sidney composed it in honour of the city of Antibes which had organized his grand wedding with Elisabeth. On that day he was "King for a Day," and the world's press reported this celebration. It was the event that attracted all the celebrities of the Côte d'Azur in the summer of 1951. In a carriage lent by the principality of Monaco, Sidney and Elisabeth were paraded down the streets to the town hall of Antibes in Juan-les-Pins, accompanied by a huge procession. Paris Match wrote: "Sidney Bechet, in celebration of his marriage on August 17 led his wife Elisabeth Ziegler into a deafening black and white carnival. Instead of yelling, 'Finally alone!' when leaving the town hall after the ceremony, he yelled out joyfully, 'Finally all together!'

All of their jazz friends had followed the syncopated procession in which the balding head of Picasso could be seen among the many free spirits from Montmartre, including pigeons in cages carried by four Black men; little Salt; Annette, Pepper's daughter; Suzanne Blum; the American vice-consul; the mayor of Cannes, some schoolchildren, and an unexpected group from the Directoire Hairdressers. The stylish thing was to be both fashionable and barbaric at the same time, solemn and bebop, as shown in Wagner's wedding march played in different keys by Thomas and his Merry Boys, by Benny Bennet and by Claude Luter in the tempo of *Saint James Infirmary*. Three kilometres of frenzy and masquerade ended up at the *Vieux Colombier* in Juan-les-Pins where a sumptuous gift awaited the newly married couple: a gold saxophone. To thank his friend, Sidney danced bebop,

cheered on by the wildest of the guests present: Mistinguett[30]."
Moustache, who was in Luter's orchestra, wrote: "There was the
mayor, the prefect, the top members of Parliament, Mistinguett
who danced the Charleston, a carriage lent by the municipality
of Monaco to transport the married couple, a two-metre long
soprano saxophone carried by pages, and eleven bands on floats
serenading the public; on other floats there were girls dressed as
barmaids distributing rum to the crowd.. From fifty miles around
ravenous people came to gorge on lunch. They must have stuffed
themselves on food for a fortnight. I was fed up pretty soon. I
didn't like this masquerade. It was too much. Bechet's apotheosis
turned into a nightmare, at the 'Big Comedy' of the down-and-
outs. I left. I wanted to be alone, far from the people partying, the
streamers and confetti, to think about a different Bechet, one who
flew, like a skylark, above our orchestra, on an amazing soprano
sax, as light as these festivities were heavy. To our friend, our
brother, our junior. To the 'Old Negro' of 20 years[31]."

The Olympia

From 1953 my father gradually stopped working with Claude
Luter's orchestra and started playing with André Réwéliotty, a
clarinettist instead Bechet and Luter were both forceful characters
and this started to create tension between the two. Working
together every day for years and going on long tours isn't easy for
anybody because it's so exhausting and tensions can erupt at any
moment. Any musician who has been on the road knows what
I mean. André Réwéliotty was really in love with Bechet and he
had a soft, understanding personality which made it easy for him

30. *Paris Match*, August 1951.
31. *Moustache, Tambour battant*, Paris, Julliard, 1975, pp. 96-97.

to get along with my father. I saw him several times at the house when I was a child. He and his band went with him to all the galas and recording sessionsright up to the end.

The pianist Yannick Singery worked about eight years with him and he became a friend of the family, coming often to dinner at our house. My father greatly appreciated him as a piano player and we can see a hint of this in *Jazz Jamboree* filmed in the Arènes de Lutèce in 1953: "For me, Sidney Bechet is without a doubt the musician who has interested me the most, and among those I've played with, he is the one who impressed me the most. For us little French amateur musicians, the idea of being able to play with him was staggering. It wasn't something we expected when we started playing jazz… and Sidney, despite the chasm between him and us, always seemed interested in what we were doing. I remember when I played he would come up to me during my choruses. He'd give me some encour-agement and really seemed to be interested in what we were doing. I don't know if he liked it or not, but he gave the impression of being interested. He never seemed to have his mind elsewhere or not to be listening to us. His presence spurred us on, of course… we even panicked in the beginning! But little by little, seeing that things were going pretty well, and he seemed

André Reweliotty

Sidney and André Réwéliotty's band. 1956.

to enjoying working with us, we relaxed and got in the habit of playing together, which made everything a lot easier... but not at the beginning![32]"

My father toured a lot with André Réwéliotty's band to galas and concerts all over France, with Claude Wolff as the road manager. The repertoire included songs from popular artists. He recorded hits from Georges Brassens, like *La Cane de Jeanne* and *Brave Margot*, always reinterpreted in the pure New Orleans style, as well as *La Complainte des infidels de Mouloudji* with a beautiful brass arrangement in the 'Jungle' style inspired by Ellington.

Assured of his fame and the appreciation he inspired, papa was, nevertheless, distrustful of competition. He did not take anything for granted and he knew that he had to keep an eye out for possible rivals. Paris at that time had become a veritable El Dorado for American musicians. In 1953 the clarinettist Albert Nicholas and the saxophonist Benny Waters had

32. *Ibid.*, pp. 190-191.

both come over. Benny was checking out all the clubs in the capital and when his time came to play at the *Vieux Colombier*, my father's stomping ground, he made the mistake of playing the soprano saxophone and being a hit. When my father was told of this a few days later, he went to meet Benny Waters in a discrete, neutral place to spell things out. He pulled out his revolver which he always carried, and pretended to polish it as he looked in the man's eyes and told him in a menacing voice: "You see, I never thought I'd have to use this here![33]" The man didn't move, but he decided to concentrate on the tenor saxophone and the clarinet.

1955 was an important year for papa when Vogue Records decided to celebrate its millionth album and organized a free concert at the Olympia where they would publicly give him a Gold Disc to crown his

career. This big Parisian music hall had opened the previous year and its reputation grew little by little. It became the temple of popular music in Paris, and jazz had its place in it. The concert was the final event in the week featuring Georges Brassens. My father didn't take into account how famous he was: by the end of the afternoon the announcement of the free concert attracted a big crowd around the Olympia. At the appointed hour, the concert began. It was hard to describe the tension as too many spectators arrived, and those who were refused entry began to destroy property. Despite the arrival of the police, the situation turned into a riot, but this did not stop my father from playing in top form accompanied by Luter's and Réwéliotty's bands The clamour for him to play. *Les Oignons* caused complete pandemonium, yet the audience miraculously quietened down

---

33. *John Chilton, op. cit., p. 267.*

Receiving the Gold Disc award with Claude Luter and André Réwéliotty at the Olympia. Paris. 1955.

when Charles Delaunay brought out the Gold Disc to present to my father with photographers' flashguns going off all around. The first artist to have caused the destruction of seats at the Olympia the year before was Gilbert Bécaud, but after Bechet's concert the great hall was thoroughly ransacked. The jovial director, Bruno Coquatrix, just shrugged his shoulders, but he sent a bill to Vogue Records to cover the cost of repairs totalling 500,000 francs (£500) at that time!

My father commented on this disc which represented a life entirely devoted to music: "I have a little secret. When I arrived home after the concert, I was like a little kid who had received a present that was too big to hold, and my heart was so full that I had to go hide in a corner and cry. From time to time I like to go look at my disc in the cranny where I put it, just like that, for a half hour, and it makes me so happy all over again.[34]"

Papa was one of the major artistes to perform at the Olympia in the fifties. He must have done about 20 shows there. The history of this Parisian music hall is often mentioned in the press, and for each commemoration, I notice that Sidney Bechet's name is never mentioned. I find this incomprehensible and unjust.

Passport to Paradise

Throughout these years my father continued to compose superb ballads like those that had established his reputation

when he first arrived in France. *Passport to Paradise* and *Premier Bal* (First Ball) are examples of this and count among his best. But studio recordings do not always do them justice, as the trumpet player Roland Hug points out: "Everybody talks to you about *Petite Fleur*... if only

Sidney Bechet , André Réwéliotty and Marcel Bornstein, 1956.

---

34. *L'Histoire de Sidney Bechet*, Album cover, Vogue SB2 a&b.

Sidney and André Réwéliotty's band.

they could go beyond this hype and simply listen to *Passport to Paradise* every evening! Forget the organs in the background and just listen to Sidney. Well, believe me, that made my evening, it was wild! You gotta listen to this. Unfortunately, it was only recorded once by Vogue as an ordinary album and that's the only way we can hear it now. It should have had a recording of a dozen concerts where he played *Passport to Paradise*: the song's title says it all. It was great![35]..."

For *Premier Bal* you absolutely have to see and hear the version he played for Jean-Christophe Averty in 1958 for television. He was accompanied by the Claude Bolling Trio and it is certainly the best-known documentary of my father that remains. It shows the exceptional intensity of both his presence and his talent for interpretation. In 1957 my father celebrated his 60th

35. Jean-Roland Hippenmeyer, *Sidney Bechet*, p. 216-217.

Sidney Bechet — Passport to Paradise

Louise Carletti, Sidney Bechet, 59th anniversary. Paris. 1956.

Sidney and Daniel. 60th anniversary. Garches. 1957.

birthday and Vogue made a big deal of it when they brought out adverts saying "Happy Birthday Sidney! Vogue Records wish you another sixty years of success!!"

For his last summer season in 1958 at the *Vieux Colombier* at Juan-les-Pins my father had Moustache's band to accompany him, with Michel Attenouit on the second soprano and Géo Daly on the vibraphone. Moustache had a dazzling memory of the event: "He still had his genius. It's a shame that they didn't record Bechet in 1958 at Juan-les-Pins playing with my band. Some evenings we reached the heights. And yet, coming down off the stage, Bechet seemed wrung out, with a dry cough. He constantly complained about a stomach ulcer he had been trying to treat for years and years. He saw it all right. He was at the end of his life. It wasn't the ulcer that carried him off in the end. He died the following year completely gutted with lung cancer.[36]"

He had his last session for Vogue Records in December, and it was one of the most original that he ever did. Already very ill, he went into the studio with an informal band, an all-stars team with the soprano and trombone backed up by a Hammond organ. The colour of tone was renewed with the old Negro spirituals and this was used to record a few Christmas carols. My father played one last time at the *Nuit de Jazz* at the Salle Wagram in Paris with this same group of musicians and that is how he wrapped up his career. He didn't pick up his saxophone again and he died the following spring on May 14, 1959, the day of his sixty-second birthday. His last piano player, Yannick Singery, said, "It seems to me that the last time I saw him was at a gala we gave in Quimper. He was already in bad shape and we were impressed by his physical

36. Moustache, *op. cit.*, p. 203.

condition but aware of the effort he was making not just to play but to hang in there… After Sidney's departure and the very big gap that left, I told myself that one of the things we always regret when somebody's gone is the feeling we should have been closer to them, that perhaps we didn't share their existence enough and that, finally, we didn't really know them well enough.[37]"

His agent Charles Delaunay, who was also the director of the magazine Jazz Hot and probably one of the men who best knew my father, spoke to him in his editorial: "You know that we love you, and you are leaving only friends behind. And I am not thinking only about the musicians you gave so much to, but also to the taxi drivers, the waiters in cafés and even those who, passing you on the street, recognized Sidney Bechet and without thinking, like an old friend, held out their hand and you shook theirs without hesitation, with that good-naturedness and simplicity that was always yours. You leave us at the height of your career, universally recognized as one of the Greats of Jazz.[38]"

Cinema and Musical Comedy

My father loved the cinema and I inherited this taste from him. One of his favorite actors was Marlon Brando. One day he met him in a hotel. He was very young. It was at the time that he was doing *A Streetcar Named Desire* which takes place in New Orleans. He must have been interested in jazz because Brando recognized my father and they talked for awhile. Then in the seventies, Brando was shot the film *Last Tango in Paris* which caused something of a scandal. In one scene I was surprised to find a photo of my father, in full view, taken at the *Vieux Colombier* and pinned up in the

37. Jean-Roland Hippenmeyer, *Sidney Bechet*, p. 191.
38. *Ibid.*, p. 147.

hero's apartment.

In a strange coincidence, there was another great American actor that my father was close to: Kirk Douglas. They met in a club on 52ⁿᵈ Street in New York when he was making the film *Young Man with a Horn*, a fictionalised biography of the horn player Bix Beiderbecke. Harry James, the trumpet player, did the sound track.

The history of cinema has known a parallel development to that of jazz, even if the cinema has unfortunately underestimated the importance of what was then new music. Jazz has often been no more than a foil. Not having made a top musical career in the USA, my father hardly ever appeared in American films. You can see him briefly in *Moon Over Harlem,* made in 1939. He played himself playing at a party and I have the pleasure of seeing my father when he was young. Nevertheless, his first appearance on film is from 1930 when he played in the Berlin-Babelsberg studios for the film *Einbrecher* (Burglars). Here he played in Berlin at the Haus Vaterland and you can catch a glimpse of him in his "New Yorkers" band while the sound track plays a clarinet solo that can only be him. The visual image is rather disappointing because he only plays the basics.

Things changed when my father came to France after the war. Apart from the newsreels that still exist in the cinema archives, there is a first film in colour shot in 1951 during his carnivalesque wedding in Antibes Juan-les-Pins. The following year *Saluti e bachi* (Love and Kisses in English; *La Route du Bonheur* in French) was made and you can see a crowd of musicians, one of whom is Louis Armstrong with his all-stars along with my father who is accompanied by Claude Luter, and it's all beautifully filmed. Then in 1953, you can see him in a flop entitled *Made in France.* The movie has aged very poorly but he plays a majestic version of *Big Chief,* one of his best compositions. This film has been lost and should remain so. The following year there was a movie, *Piédalu député,* that was filmed in the Arènes de Lutèce which does my father justice and in which he gives a concert accompanied by André Réwéliotty. They play two excellent versions of *Royal Garden Blues* and *Saint Louis Blues*, and the image is superb.

In 1955 there were two full length detective feature films.. In the first, *Blues, L'Inspecteur connait la Musique* (The Inspector knows the Music), the plot involves Claude Luter killing my father; and in the second thriller, *Série Noire* (Chain of Disasters), he plays the simple role of a cabaret musician alongside Robert Hossein and Erich von Stroheim. Far from being cinematic masterpieces, these full length movies manage to take us into the atmosphere of the 1950s thriller, and they also show a realistic picture of my father and his sparkling style on the soprano sax. Finally, the last film he made was in 1956: *Ah! Quelle Equipe* (Ah! What a Team!). It was in colour and Bechet has a big role; that of Candy, a brilliant Black saxophone player who is homesick for his native New Orleans and who ends up acquiring a Show Boat to take on a trip. He is depicted as a kind of Uncle Tom and it is rather uncomfortable to watch this today, but his energy and presence make up for this weakness. This was, of course, still the era of colonialism and there is an allusion to this in a scene with Noël Roquevert. The music was written in collaboration with Gérard Calvi, and there is a very beautiful rendition of *Dowden by the Old Mill* played by Réwéliotty for a Henry Spade broadcast, *La joie de vivre*.

Finally in 1958, the last year my father was active, he was caught on film three times by Jean-Christophe Averty. The first time was in the studio 105 at ORTF where, with Claude Bolling, he plays *Premier Bal* from an anthology, as well as *Saint Louis Blues*. The last documentaries come from the Cannes Festival which took place in July of that year. Averty preserved a presentation of *I've Found a New Baby* with Réwéliotty, where

*Albert Nicholas, Sidney Bechet, Sammy Price, Teddy Buckner, 7
Arvell Shaw at a concert at Knokke le Zoute, Belgium. 1958.*

you can see that my father had grown weaker physically but he plays a fantastic rendition of *Sweet Georgia Brown* played with an American All-Stars team around him composed of Teddy Buckner on the trumpet, Vic Dickenson on the trombone, Sammy Price on the piano, Arvell Shaw on the double bass, and Roy Eldridge on the drums- and boy do they smoke! With such a distinguished cast of musicians, the New Orleans style is there in all its glory. It's a real treasure.

At the end of 1957, my father had the opportunity to leave the club and concert routine with André Réwéliotty's band and take part in the production of a stage musical written by Pascal Bastia. Originally entitled *My Louisiana*, it was later rebaptized *New Orleans*. It was produced at the beginning of 1958 at the Theâtre de l'Etoile. Yves Montand wrote a note in the programme: "New Orleans was to records... what Greta Garbo was to the movies... and then you came among us... since we're all a bit proud of our country, we were proud that you were called Bechet like someone born in Orleans, France. And you played jazz for us; that's what we call this music in "Old Orleans" just as we do in "New Orleans" and in the whole world... You came and you stayed. Thank you, Sidney." Staging this project was apparently very difficult, and there was a lot of discord on the musical level between the librettist, Pascal Bastia and my father. He had dug out melodies from his enormous repertoire, in particular Creole ones, for this musical, but the show was criticised. As with his ballet, *La Nuit est une sorcière* (The Night is a Witch) the general public did not appreciate their idol in such a context. The show never took off and it closed after five weeks as a monumental flop which seriously demoralized my father- and Pascal Bastia spent several years recovering from the financial disaster. A lawsuit was filed between the two protagonists and it was Vogue Records which paid the cost which put an end to the legal action. The production probably was too big, requiring at least 75 actors on stage including a debutant by the name of Jacques Higelin, Mattie Petter, the future Virginia Vee, an incompetent orchestra and a six-man jazz band directed by my father.

The weekly Paris Match wrote up this version of the facts that was worthy of a soap opera entitled: "'Sidney Bechet, the jazz magician says good-bye to his musicians to the tune of *Les Oignons*.' The curtain falls. The staff hand out paper onions to 500 spectators who join together to sing *Les Oignons*, the final song of the first act of the musical, *New Orleans*. A half hour goes by. The curtain does not go back up. The theatre director of L'Etoile comes out and says: 'you will be reimbursed.' Boos and yells turn to anger. At the stage door, with his white hair, raincoat collar turned up, Sidney Bechet slowly gets into his black Lincoln. Ten minutes earlier, the seven musicians from the musical knocked on his dressing-room door: 'We haven't been paid for eight days. We can't continue to play.' 'Me, neither,' says Bechet, 'I haven't been paid for four weeks. Let's get out of here!' However, this dark story had started well. One day at Garches, on the steps of a stone-built house, sat a boy playing with a clarinet. 'Could you show me Mr. Bechet's house, please?' Daniel Bechet, four years old, points out his parents' house to the stranger. In the dining room sipping Coca-Cola, Sidney fiddled with the stones of his two fetish rings, emerald on the right hand and diamond on the left. Jacqueline, his wife, was painting her nails. 'My name is Bastia,' said the visitor. 'Would you like the lead role in my next musical?' 'Okay,' said Bechet, 'but only if I like the music.'

'If you don't like it, you can rewrite it!' In three months Bechet rewrote it. He recruited one of the Peters Sisters as a partner and seventy-five actors. On December 24, the day of the opening, there was not a cent left. They were counting on the day's takings. They were catastrophic: 2 million francs per week. After paying the production costs, there remained only 100,000 francs (£100) per week for the actors. Bechet was to earn 50,000 francs a day but after a run of five weeks he had only made 120,000 francs. Then the black Lincoln veered off course on the Rue de Sèvres.

Sidney looked for some sort of consolation, so he returned to the scene of his former glory years, the *Vieux Colombier*. It was like his own home. In 1949 he had the rats of Saint-Germain dancing the boogie. Fortune followed. 4 million albums sold in 10 years. Bechet, the son of a Black shoe maker in New Orleans was a multimillionaire who led a modest suburban life style. His only passion was collecting state of the art cameras which he never used. Here, in his honour the band struck up *Les Oignons*, but this time it almost made him cry.[39]"

39. *Paris Match*, February 1958.

La Chanson d'Omar (Omar's Song) and Soleil Africain (African Sun)

When papa moved to France in stages in 1949 it was not by chance. It was the result of deep reflection. The phenomenal artistic success he experienced, especially since it was so unexpected, encouraged his quest for meaning, something that was an important impetus in his life. In his book *Treat it Gently*, he opened up and was completely frank, once more making a reference to that mythical grandfather who seemed to have guided him all his life. "One night, I was playing at the *Vieux Colombier* in Paris when this story burst into my memory and will haunt me to my dying day: the story of my grandfather, Omar. And I started telling it again as I played on my soprano saxophone, as if I were rolling out its vibrant and sombre melody. I told it again, as it bubbled up from the depth of my memories. I saw it all again as it played out in my mind. I let the story take me over. I see the tall, powerful shadow

Sidney at the Vieux Colombier. *Paris. 1950.*

of my grandfather. It was as if he were speaking through my lips, as if I had identified myself with him. At the same time I asked myself the question: 'Why am I here? In France… in Paris ?'The answer came immediately. France is closer to Africa than is America. I had always wanted to be as close as possible to Africa. That's how my mind functioned, and it was the atmosphere that I had always wanted to bathe in; my grandfather represented Africa for me. My grandfather *was*

Africa. So for me, this was a first step to my return home. And I longed so much for this homecoming.[40]"

On the spoken level, things were clearly said. On the musical level, I think they were, too. The best illustration of this is a fantastic composition that he recorded in 1949 at the very beginning of his contract with Vogue, with only the drummer Kenny Clarke to accompany him. The piece is called *American Rhythm* and it is a duo for soprano saxophone and the drums. I think it's extraordinary! Both of them give their all.My father improvised for three minutes on a single chord with the vigour and bite of his heyday, and he is supported and pushed along past any obstacles by Kenny's polyrhythmic play and fantastic drive. Remember, Kenny the inventor of bop drumming. It's as if we are in a voodoo ritual, or witnesses to the return to the drums on Congo Square, hearing something by Omar! It is a jazz masterpiece which perfectly illustrates this return to Africanness which my father preached at that time. If you can consider that this was also a major preoccupation with the drummers and percussionists of the bop style, it makes you wonder. Finally, and this is probably the most troubling for me, this is probably where I feel like I am the trustee of a history connected through invisible threads. I too became a percussionist drummer under the guidance of Kenny Clarke. Leaving from Congo Square, the flame travelled up to me and I believe I can say that I, too, have tried to develop this heritage in all the ethnic music with which I have collaborated.

Improvisation in three minutes quite spontaneously, *American Rhythm* is a complete success which contrasts with the other more or less fruitful attempts by my father to pay

40. Sidney Bechet, *LaMusique c'est ma vie*, Paris, La Table Ronde, 1977, pp. 70-71.

homage to his mythically remembered ancestor. This piece is a perfect illustration of it, and it seems to be addressed to each of us: "For me, it is Omar who began the new music. Well, perhaps he didn't exactly start it. There were people who were playing and beating the rhythm behind him and there were even more people before. But it was Omar who was the inspiration of the melody, this new music. Before Omar, there was the rhythm, but after him there was the melody. He is the one who started this new melodic idea, and all the good musicians have been magnifying it since then, changing it a bit, adding parts, opening a new direction for it to follow and evolve. But if you are a musician, and if you are a good musician, it's all variations on Omar's song that you're singing… and wherever it's played, you have to hear him who begins far back in time, far before you. It is the drum that they beat on Congo Square, and the chant that begins on the plantations, rising up over the trees. The good musician plays *with* this chant in him, and he also plays *after* the chant has taken flight. He tries to perfect it. And whatever he plays, it's always the same music, that grand inspiration that began over there, in the South.[41]"

La Nuit est une sorcière
(The Night is a Witch)

An important thing happened in 1951 when my father was contacted to write a score for a ballet whose storyline was based on the master-slave relationship and which was not unlike the story he himself had been dreaming for a long time of creating. He wrote a synopsis: "The title of the ballet was 'The Night is a Witch'(*La Nuit est une sorcière*), and it talks about a guy who

41. *Ibid*, pp. 253-254.

Performance of The Night is a Witch *ballet. Paris. 1954.*

walks in his sleep and his parents are terrified because when he walks at night, he climbs up to the attic and walks on the top of the roof. They're terribly afraid and the father decides to try to stop him if possible. So the father, the mother and the fiancée stay up and wait on events: they see him walking and they wait. When he arrives in the attic, his father tries to talk to him. The son throws darts at a target until he finally throws a dart at his father and kills him. Then he kills his mother: she tried to treat him as a child and she takes a piece of string and makes shapes with it (it's the game of cat's cradle). He takes the string and chokes her with it. And he kills his fiancée, too. And every time he kills, it's a spirit, that of his servant, a young Black man who dances and incites him to do all these things in his sleep. And he thinks his servant really is his servant, whereas he, the servant, is the one who commands his master and makes him commit all these crimes. And when there is finally no one else to kill, he tries to play with the string, but he realizes he has forgotten how. So when the Black man plays this game that his young master no longer knows how to play, the master can now only kill himself[42]…"

---

42. *Ibid.*, pp. 249-250.

The librettist André Coffrant explained why he met my father:

"I always thought that this story took place in one of those grand Victorian houses, surrounded by cotton fields, in Georgia or Carolina. That's why when I searched my memory to understand what had pushed me to go the *Vieux Colombier* and pitch this idea of a ballet to Bechet, I see it only as logical and natural. Bechet is one of those people who don't need to understand to love; feeling deeply is enough for them. Naturally I went to the source. A few days later, I understood, and even more so when he returned from the United States and I heard him play a duet on the piano, the score from the ballet. Bechet had assimilated the main idea and had written it in his language, music. Later I spent time with Bechet on several occasions. I watched him play; I went to his recording sessions and his rehearsals. Recently, I remember he recorded *Clouds*, after the death of Django Reinhardt (the three-fingered gypsy guitarist). I saw him listen attentively to the melody which he didn't know. He then went off into a corner of the studio, blew into his instrument for a bit, then came back to the orchestra and played not only the melodic theme, but also improvised on his soprano saxophone. He led the orchestra into a distant melody of which only he knew the secret, hunched over his instrument which he leaned on a wooden step , he blew until he was out of breath. That day I understood that Bechet, every time he plays, is tempted by a unique pleasure. He becomes one with his instrument and the melody that emerges is a sort of moan under a noonday sun. Bechet is one of those beings who always walks in full light; the song of the earth, of those who labour on it and of those who enjoy it- they are all within his reach. The essence of music not only speaks to his mind, it also invades his guts and rises to his head to affirm the abdication of his whole being.. Bechet's composition for *The Night is a Witch* makes me think- I swear! - of childhood. It is as cruel as a child who stamps his foot and wallops his playmate who doesn't reply, but instead becomes pale, then green, then all of a sudden, after freezing in death's arms, crumbles. From sleep-walking until death, there is only the ray of light, and that is something Bechet understood.[43]"

To get back to this story which resonates closely with the story of papa's origins, I would like to quote a letter from Dr. Desmond Flower who was the London publisher of *Treat it Gently*, and who also tried to uncover the mystery that infused its poetics: "Bechet, among all the jazz musicians I have personally known, was the only one who was a total introvert... I saw Bechet play, and I deliberately use the word 'saw', for the first time in 1931 and from that moment until the end of his life, I did not see any notable changes. On the musical level he lived completely in a world of his own. There were women, and fights with the police, and so on, but for his music, he imposed an incredible discipline on himself as well as on others who played with him, sometimes successfully, sometimes not. When he finished a set, he was in a trance and the public did not really exist for him. He knew what he wanted to do, and knew very well if he had accomplished it. If he succeeded, the applause didn't mean much to him; if he failed, there was nothing else to say. For a man of such passionate nature and who could produce such powerful music and with such an impressive imagination, keeping up such fierce discipline must have been hard. I believe fantasy must have been his safety valve: when he wasn't composing splendid themes, his fertile imagination swept along his dreams in a world of twilight. In so many ways the extraordinary and moving ballet which he composed towards the end of his life resembled the fantastical story of his grandfather, chased to his death in the swamps of the Deep South. When I once asked him

43. LP Sidney Bechet, Album cover, Vogue CLVLX 255.

to tell me the story of the ballet in his own words, he did so in a very deep voice and with a depth of feeling that let me know that he was once again practically in a trance. How true was the story of his grandfather? I have no idea; but the terrible story of the chase and the escape into the darkness, with the chance of an inevitable death- whether it was true or not- fascinated him. It chained him up and he had spent his existence trying to find the person who could set him free; someone who, perhaps, could explain to him why when he spoke, he spoke too much; and why when someone wanted to know how King Oliver was, he would give such an ambiguous answer. It was like talking to Cocteau.[44]"

The Hill of the Delta

Although the première of *The Night is a Witch* took place at the Palais de Chaillot in Paris, it was not the hit everyone expected and the ballet turned out to be too expensive to produce, so it was quickly taken off. Of course, the public completely ignored this work which my father held dear to his heart. Those who came to the show were disconcerted because they were hearing their idol in a completely unusual context. The critics did not pay any attention to this effort to bring jazz and a symphony orchestra together, even though this sort of thing would become commonplace in the decades to come.

But it took a lot to discourage my father. He plunged back, heart and soul, into his initial project, helped in it by the arranger-composer Gérard Calvi. Let us remember that in 1928 he wrote *Negro Rhapsody* in homage to the Black American slaves, but it was not followed up. His desire to have a major work dedicated

44. Jean-Roland Hippenmeyer, *Sidney Bechet*, Geneva, Tribune Éditions, 1980, p. 155.

to his grandfather Omar lasted throughout the decades and resulted in the composition of *Mississippi Rhapsody* around 1954. He conceived it in the form of a rhapsodic ballet for soprano saxophone and symphony orchestra in eight vignettes, with orchestration by Gérard Calvi. The project stayed shelved until Vogue decided to save it. By that time, my father had passed away and it was Claude Luter on the soprano sax who recorded the work which they rebaptized *The Hill of the Delta*. The story takes place in New Orleans with a slave owner's house, a church and a river boat on the Mississippi flowing through luxuriant bayous. A love story between two slaves is the highlight of the story and echoes Omar's experience. The tragedy is referred to in a passage entitled *The Slave Revolt*, but the work ends on a more soothing note that is a bit sugary, probably under the influence of the arranger Gérard Calvi. The score was played only one time in a concert in Monte Carlo soon after its composition in 1964, and part of the ballet was presented on television in 1968 with the star dancer from the *Opéra de Paris* Claude Bessy. On his side, proudly recognizing this work written in collaboration with Sidney Bechet, Gérard Calvi toyed with the idea of presenting it at the Montreux Festival in Switzerland in the 1980s. The saxophone player Manu Dibango had been chosen to interpret it, but the project fell through. It was not until more than thirty years later that this second ballet was talked about again.

In 1997, in New York, to mark the centennial of my father's birth, a big jazz band performed *The Hill of the Delta* at the Carnegie Hall using a modern arrangement with the saxophone player Dick Oatts, a disciple of John Coltrane. Later in 2000, still in America, the original work orchestrated by Gérard Calvi was

Sidney with the dancers in his ballet. Juan-les-Pins. 1951.

played and danced for the first time in Eugene, Oregon. The show was done in a concert with the theme "Americans and Europe," and it was Bob Wilber who interpreted the soprano-sax solos with Eugene's entire symphony orchestra. In an interview, the American producer for this concert explained that he had watched to the two ballets, *The Night is a Witch* and *The Hill of the Delta*, but that he preferred the second by far because the soprano saxophone was much more present. Also, he was surprised that such an ambitious work, written by one of the great American jazz musicians, had been completely passed over, and that it had never found its place in Bechet's adoptive country, and that there had been no attentive ear to make such an important work live. For the man in the street, as for the informed musicologist, Bechet is known for *Les Oignons* and that's that, which is a shame. The absence of curiosity seems to be the rule and it is mass culture that counts. Political correctness is the guideline and when someone submits a project that is out of line, a lot of courage is needed to achieve it. This second ballet which occupied the last years of my father's life shows a desire to retrace a long road, as if he had returned to the starting point: "All that I still want is music, because all the beauty in the world is in music. Omar's voice is in it, and the voice of the young girl, and the rustling wind in Africa, and the cries coming from Congo Square, and the superb cacophony of the voices the day the slaves were freed. The blues and the spirituals, the memories and the waiting, and the suffering and the gazing up at heaven as night fell, all this is in the music.[45]"

45. Sidney Bechet, *op. cit.*, p. 271.

Secret garden

I a m half French and half American, and I have a bit of the same feeling as my father had, that of being, how can I put it… a bit uprooted, not having a home port . Am I Black? Am I White? Maybe I'm Black. My father was mixed, my mother, White. I have the good and the bad temperament of both sides. My American mother-in-law (who was Black) used to enjoy telling me: "You have a Black temper." My mother once told me that I had inherited a lot from my father, both his sense of melody and of rhythm, but, like him, I also had a problem with communication. I am rather introverted. I also have his tenacity which sometimes helps me complete projects that I have undertaken. I have stored up a lot of memories of my father which have helped me and supported me at certain moments in my life and I often have the feeling that he is protecting me. In life, I have always done things by myself, but I also know that whatever roads I have taken at certain moments,, the events invariably brought me closer to him.

There are accounts of my birth, and I want to mention one by Bernard Wagnière, a friend of my father's, and recorded by the journalist Roland Hippenmeyer: "Sidney was supposed to play one evening in Lausanne, at the Tabaris, and he asked me to go with him. So we went off to Lausanne and arrived at the Hôtel de la Paix where he had reserved a room. The moment we walked in, an employee from the hotel came up to Sidney, 'Monsieur Bechet, there is a telegram for you.' Well, Sidney read the telegram and his eyes started popping out of his head… I wondered: 'My god, what could be in this telegram?' You could expect anything with Sidney… and then he said it was nothing special. At that point we took the elevator, and that's where, in this small box, he tells us, 'Wow! Man! I'm a papa!'… he went wild! This was fantastic because we knew he was expecting a son…and I tell you, he took us for one of those big meals. And that night he played at the Tabaris like I had rarely heard him play before! He was overcome with such indescribable joy. It was really fantastic![46]"

To understand the relationship I had with my father, I need to quote another account by the journalist Raymond Mouly who wrote the first biography of my father just after his death in 1959.This is what my father said about me: "He's terrible. He always wants to play with my tools. At the back of the house I have a room where I tinker and make some furniture by myself. For that I have some electric saws and other tools, dangerous for a child. Well, it was with those toys there that he wanted to play. One day he had taken a pair of pliers and he had taken off all the door knobs in the house… He also liked music. He sang *Au clair de la lune* with the words, and when he heard *Les Oignons*, he kept time like a grown-up. Another

46. Jean-Roland Hippenmeyer, *Sidney Bechet*, Geneva, Tribune Éditions, 1980, p. 200.

Jacqueline and Daniel.
1955.

thing he loved was when I pretended to be a horse for him. He called it 'papa pony.' I'd get down on my hands and knees, he'd climb up on my back and we'd have fun like that until it was time for him to go and take his nap. I'd give him a kiss and that's that."

Later, my father said: "I wanted to go back to America for a long trip. I took one of my cameras and I took Daniel along. Both of us, we were going to go to where I had been born, to the school and the church and everywhere I used to go. I was going to film all that, and with my son I was going to walk in the same steps I had taken when I was young…"

These are the only accounts written by my father about me that I have found. I didn't see him often because he worked a lot, so he was rarely at home. Sometimes he was there but since he was tired, we had to let him rest. But when I had the chance to have him all to myself, it was always fun. He was very playful and affectionate with me. I can still see him take me in his arms, but I also see myself arguing with him. In between two gigs, when he was relaxing, he would take me with him and we would take a turn in the car in style. I can still smell the leather seats in his Lincoln, a big American car that made a

Sidney, Charles Delaunay and Daniel. 1957.

big impression every-where we went. We would take a walk and visit friends who would welcome us warmly. He was very proud to introduce me to them. I had the impression of being on the road with him, and at those moments I existed. At the house my father loved having friends over, many of whom were musicians. He would make Creole dishes that I honestly didn't want to taste. He would make pasta with anchovies, for example, or some other strange combinations which I did not like. When he'd come home from Paris at three in the morning after having worked all night, he would make a detour to the kitchen and prepare spaghetti with sardines or some other culinary curiosity which was supposed to come from his native New Orleans.

Papa had a habit of taking apart sophisticated objects that belonged to him. He wanted to understand how they worked. One day he took a beautiful Dunhill cigarette lighter completely apart. Once he had all the pieces laid out in front of him, he wanted to put it back together. He never succeeded.

Sidney fixing his Buescher.

He tried several times but he found himself with extra parts, and naturally the lighter no longer worked. He should never have done it with a Dunhill, but when he was asked why he persisted in doing it, he said: "I want to fix something....", although the lighter had been working perfectly. He finally took it back to the shop and asked the shopkeeper to fix it, which he did because he was Sidney Bechet. It was a good thing he didn't do this with his soprano sax - but then he knew how to fix that with a screwdriver.

I remember a nice story that shows how kind and generous he was on occasion. He owned three pairs of binoculars, one of which was rather sophisticated and could take photos, something that was rare at the time. One day a neighbour's kid, who must have been around 16 years old, stole a pair. He was a nice kid, even if he was a bit of a kleptomaniac, who was constantly following my father, and my mother noticed the theft. Two days later, there was a knock on the door. It was the kid, in tears, accompanied by his father. Very embarrassed,

Sidney, X and Daniel in Garches. 1957.

the man explained that his son had stolen a pair of binoculars. He had brought him over to give back what he had stolen and apologize. My father saw the distress in the boy's eyes and the shame of having been caught in the act. He took his binoculars back and looked straight into the boy's eyes and said: "Let that be a lesson to you! Every time you look in these binoculars, you will think about the stupid thing you did and you will relive the uncomfortable situation you are living right now!" And he gave them back to him! The boy's father said: "You have an incredible chance here, and you don't deserve it. You thank Mr Bechet because you will never have another opportunity like this in your life!" Along the same lines, my father punished me sometimes when I did something stupid, but more from fear of what could have happened to me than from desire. I used to climb in the garden because I was a turbulent child. Rather than forbid me to do it, he made me do it again so he could explain to me the danger I was exposing myself to.

That was his child-rearing technique, and I find it a good one. At that time I was often bored. I was alone a lot and curious about everything.

One day, a man we knew came by the house. It was cold because it was wintertime. When he was about tot to leave, he complained about the cold and asked to borrow something to keep him warm on the way home. My father opened his closet and told him to choose an overcoat. Now papa had just bought himself a very luxurious cashmere coat and the guy in question picked that one without hesitation. That's when my mom intervened and said: "Listen Sidney, if you want to play the good Samaritan, that's your business. But I'm gonna forbid you to lend that coat. You can offer him a more ordinary one that'll be just as good!" But if my father had been alone, I think he would have let the guy leave with his nice new cashmere coat. He didn't know how to say no. For a long time, I, too, had this over-developed sense of generosity.

One day when he wanted to order some wine, an unscrupulous wine merchant had succeeded in having him buy a ridiculous amount of wine, enough to stock a restaurant. The day of the delivery, my mother saw a big truck stopping in front of the house unloading a barrel of at least 500 litres of wine. The diameter of the barrel was so big that it would have been impossible to get through the door of the cellar. My mother told them: "I don't think that Mr Bechet has the intention of opening a restaurant." They had to fight to change the order, but the delivery man ended up leaving with his merchandise.

My mother also told me the following story. My father was shopping in Paris and he was loaded down with bags and a baguette under his arm. At one point he took a covered

Bechet with the Constabulary.

passageway and at the other end there was a policeman controlling traffic. When he arrived at the other end, the policeman raised his baton and my father believing he was going to be struck stepped back ready to defend himself,. In reality, the policeman was signalling to a car my father hadn't seen and telling it to stop. Having been accustomed to street fights in New Orleans and Chicago when he was young, my father never lost the defensive mechanism, which kicked in when he saw the raised baton. Seeing the officer so surprised by his reaction, both of them were now on the defensive. That's when a second officer came up and said to his colleague: "Stop! Don't you see that's Sidney Bechet?" The situation was resolved when papa signed autographs on their ticket pads.

Papa also loved teasing people, another of his character traits. One day my mother saw a very pretty topaz in a jewelry store and had my father look at it. He showed a certain interest, but no more than that. A week later, he went to my grand-mother's house and he told Jacqueline (my mother): "Look what I'm gonna offer to your mama. I know how much she loves jewelry!" I won't describe the look my mother made. The air was so tense that after only a few minutes he admitted that the ring was for her! One glance at those murderous-looking

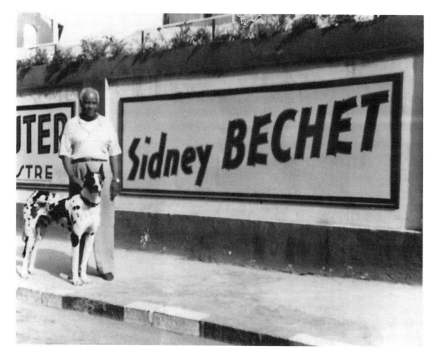

Sidney and Yank. Juan-les-Pins. 1951.

eyes and he quickly made peace.

My father had always loved big dogs, especially Great Danes. His first one, named Yank, had an important place in the household. He often slept at the foot of the stairs that led to my bedroom. I would wake up very early in the morning while everyone else still slept. One day I was hungry so I went downstairs. At the bottom I tripped over the last step and fell over Yank who was sleeping peacefully. My face bumped hard against the dog's muzzle and he woke up with a start. He began barking and making such a loud, infernal noise that he woke everybody up. I had split open my upper lip because I had fallen against his teeth, and the wound was bleeding profusely. He hadn't bitten me, but I had to be taken to the hospital for some stitches. Blinded by anger, my father screamed that he was going to kill the dog, thinking that he had tried to bite me. "I'm gonna get my gun and teach him a lesson!" he said. My mother tried to calm him down. Even the hospital doctor tried to reassure him, saying that if the Great Dane had really wanted to bite a child, his four-year-old son would no longer have been of this world. In any case, Yank had always been very gentle with me and I often played with him as if he was a big horse. Despite this, my father still wanted to kill him, so much so that my mother called Elisabeth to tell her to go get the dog and take him somewhere far from my father's ire. The Great Dane stayed quite some time at the house in Grigny because Elisabeth had grown attached to him. One day my father dropped by and when he approached the house he heard barking. He recognized his dog, but Elisabeth retorted: "No, no. That's a German Shepherd that I picked up. He's mine!" My

Sidney and a friend, house in Garches.

father wasn't fooled, but this became a game between the two of them. I still had the scar. Later, my father came home with a magnificent collie like the one in the film *Lassie Come Home*. He was very proud of him but three days later the dog jumped the fence and we never saw him again. My father believed my mother hadn't kept a good enough eye on the dog because she didn't want one, and they argued about this.

When my father was at home, he sometimes came to tuck me up in bed and he would bring a newspaper and scissors. He would open and refold the newspaper the way he wanted it in order to obtain two tubes with the pages. Then he would cut from right to left before suddenly pulling at it all, and then I would see a paper ladder. This seemed like magic to me and he'd tell me: "There you go! I'm doing this so that the angels that come to see you will be able to climb back up to heaven and take you to the world of dreams!" He would hang it on the wall. When I found myself all alone the first time, I got out of bed, tried to climb on the ladder and I tore it all up. So I asked him why I couldn't climb it and he told me: "It's not for you. You're too heavy. Angels are light. They use it as a stepping ladder to jump from your window, my little Daniel." Devastated, I returned to bed. I watched him closely when he was cutting with the scissors and I noticed that his first two fingers were yellowed by tobacco because he smoked a lot. I was intrigued because I didn't understand why his fingers were stained. In any case, my father knew how to create a dream with this ladder. It was pure poetry, and it was the little things like this that marked the child I was and the man I am.

The last days were not a lot of fun. When I saw my father, he was always lying down. I couldn't have known he was gravely ill because nobody talked to me about it. Later, Elisabeth told me about the last occasions when they were together. My father loved life, a true *bon vivant* who loved eating, and Elisabeth knew just how to make his favourite dishes to keep him with her. Having tasted them myself, I can tell you she knew how to make some delicious German recipes. But with his illness, my father had a hard time eating. Elisabeth told me that his illness caused a ring of ganglions to develop around his neck making it difficult for him to swallow, and it took him a good two hours to swallow a meal. It was horrible!

One day we were in Menton. Papa was lying down and I was bored to death. So I started playing with some matches and I set his bed cover on fire. I didn't mean to. Maybe unconsciously I must have wanted to make him get out of bed. In any case, I panicked, my father woke up and the doctor arrived – all at the

Forced peace and quiet.

same time. My father told him: "See, my son has found a radical way to treat me!"

My father died of lung cancer. He loved me a lot and I didn't understand why he looked so sad when he took me in his arms. The last time I saw him, it was a Sunday. I was watching Jean Cocteau's *Beauty and the Beast* starring Jean Marais on the television. There was a lot of tension in the house. My mother kept on telling me he was tired. Today when I happen upon this film, I think back to this day and my father's death. When he died, Elisabeth told me she was the one holding his hand. He had squeezed it really hard and whispered to her, "Daniel, Daniel... I beg you, take care of him!" Earlier she had thrown a doctor out of the room when he tried to keep on giving him injections in the foot in order to prolong his life. When he died, he weighed no more than forty kilos. That shows how much he had suffered. At that time they did not use morphine to help relieve the pain. Without this type of treatment, patients had to endure great suffering.

Towards the end, many people, especially those close to us, visited my father at Garches Hospital. But there is a troubling story that is still told today in which my father, when he was feeling his worst, had a visit from George Wein, a manager. They were close friends and at that time Wein was the founder of the Newport Festival and he managed some jazz clubs in Boston. He tells the story that my father begged him to take him back home to America. But where, I wonder? He hadn't had any contact for years with his American family. On the other hand, my close family was very present and kept a watch on all the comings and goings. George Wein repeated 'his truth' in New York in 1997, at a concert for the Bechet Bicentennial at Carnegie Hall. I taped the evening and he insists, almost forty years after his death, that my father wanted desperately and by any means to return to the United States to die. I don't know what to think, but I would say that the world of jazz in America believes this story because they find it hard to accept that my father left the United States forever and found fame and fortune in Europe. This sounds like an attempt to reclaim him.

Later, after my father's passing, other well-known people continued to come by the house to bear witness, to my mother and myself, of their affection and respect for the "Master" (that's want they called him) who continued to inspire them. They never left without stopping to pay their respects at his grave. Here are a few of them: the singer Carmen McRae, saxophone players Dexter Gordon and Johnny Griffin, drummers Max Roach, Kenny Clarke and Art Taylor, as well as the pianist and blues singer Memphis Slim. I grew up in this magical universe peopled with extraordinary musicians whose talents were only equalled by their generous spirit. Everyone had seen in my father a commitment and a total respect for music, for all kinds of music. He often said, "Music can only be offered to those who love and appreciate it. That's probably why so many musicians become like swine. One of them signs a contract and goes play somewhere. He wants to make music but nobody cares what he plays. It's like that in many places.. Music must be a total gift. But you need to have someone ready to accept and respect that gift.[47]"

Montand, Piaf and Mariano

At the time that my father played at the *Vieux Colombier* in Paris with Claude Luter, there were a lot of big names in show business and the arts who frequented the place. They were what we would

47. Sidney Bechet, *La Musique c'est ma vie*, Paris, La Table Ronde, 1977, p. 267.

call "the beautiful people" today. Yves Montand was one of them. He was completely in awe of my father, especially his rhythmic perfection. When it was his time to sing, Montand would include a lot of up-tempo songs influenced by jazz and the Charleston. He developed his work along these lines and the musicians who accompanied him were all seasoned jazzmen like Henri Crolla on the guitar, Bob Castella on the piano, Hubert Rostaing on the clarinet, to name a few. He was a workaholic. When he rehearsed his show, it had to be exact and everything timed to the last millimetre. This was the age of the music hall, and Montand got his inspiration from the Americans whose fluent style he admired, especially the great jazzmen like my father, Louis Armstrong and Ella Fitzgerald. Before becoming a confirmed French star, my father was first a well-known character in the Saint-Germain-des-Près quarter. He played there every night and hobnobbed with celebrities, particularly Juliette Gréco and Marcel Mouloudji with whom he recorded the famous song *La Complainte des infidels*.

Papa also loved musical comedies. He was buddies with Luis Mariano. He admired his sunny-warm throaty tenor voice, his musical sensibility and the passion which filled him when he belted out one of those superb songs written by Francis Lopez. They constantly played *petanque* (the outdoor bowling game) together when they were in Southern France. They had a lot of fun together because Mariano was someone who was always affable and good-humoured. My father also appreciated and was good friends with the lyric singer Dario Moreno. They had much in common, as do all artists who have been around the track a few times before hitting it big. They both carried a revolver, and they kept banknotes in small denominations rolled up in a sock which they carried on their person. They didn't trust banks.

My father also liked female singers, especially Edith Piaf. He felt that she perfectly personified French song, and he sometimes told musicians, "There you have it! Your Blues singer!" My father was making an allusion to those White singers who tried to copy Bessie Smith or Billie Holiday, something he found ridiculous. For him, Piaf was a sort of French blues singer. In the same way, he loved the Portuguese singer Amalia Rodrigues, the queen of *fado*. He had once said to my mother that for those listening, the language is not very important because there is an underlying common language, emotion and roots, and that was her style of blues.

Claude Wolff, Petula Clark's husband, was my father's road manager when he was with André Réwéliotty's band. He told people what a practical joker my father was: "Sidney was a little rascal. During one of those famous summer tours, in a hotel where he had the impression that he had been particularly badly received, the dinner had not been good, and he decided to take revenge. He went out to his car and got a tin of fishing maggots, the ones that turn into big blue flies, and proceeded to lay them conscientiously in all the drawers of his room, saying, 'Okay, old man, you're gonna see, in eight, ten days, this place is gonna be perfect!' So he left all that in all the furniture and all over the place… something a fifteen or eighteen-year-old kid would do, but I found it rather funny![48]" Claude Wolff told another story: when he bought his big car, the green one, the one with a miniature soprano sax on the hood, he had a compass installed inside. Everybody laughed but Sidney said, "with that I won't get lost in Paris![49]" This was the time he was doing a lot of touring and there were many

48. Roland Hippenmeyer, *Sidney Bechet*, p. 194.
49. *Ibid.*, p. 198.

Sidney Bechet, André Réwéliotty, X, and Gilbert Bécaud.

Annie Cordy and Sidney Bechet.

Luis Mariano and Sidney Bechet.

stories that circulated. One evening in Evian all the musicians had gone to one of the biggest restaurants in the town and my father had ordered salmon. In the fifties it was a rare dish and very expensive. Sidney ate his salmon and when the waiters brought him the bill, he started and said, "I hope your safe is well refrigerated for the night! Seeing the people did not understand, he added, "for salmon that costs more than gold, you should put it in a safe or somebody's gonna steal it from you!"

My mother sometimes came with my father when he went on tours. One time they were going to play in a place where they were paid less than the going rate. The concert was supposed to be in two sets. After the break, my father refused to go back for the second set. The organizer panicked because there was a big audience waiting and getting angry that the artists weren't already back. He had to raise the fee before my father would do the second set. He was very firm; he had his way of being heard. Another anecdote, this time showing how he respected his public, deals with a day after he had a fall. His knee was very swollen and hurt him a lot. He limped and walked with great difficulty. Because of this he had my mother carry all his things for him, and she felt he was taking advantage of her. When it was time for the evening concert, she watched with amazement as Sidney walked on stage without the slightest trace of a limp. He played without a hitch and at the end, rather vexed, my mother said to him, "I'm happy to see that your knee is much better!" My father answered: "The public didn't come to a concert to see Sidney Bechet limp!" In fact, he was suffering a lot, but through willpower he had managed to mask the problem despite the pain he was going through.

Armstrong, Duke, Hampton and others

When I was very young, I met a lot of great names in jazz the simple mention of which would blow a musician's mind. From the age of three and a half (my first memories), I saw a parade of names go through the family house in Garches without being aware of their notoriety. I saw people like the clarinetist Albert Nicholas, Mezz Messrow, André Réwéliotty, my father's agent Charles Delaunay (the son of painters Robert and Sonia Delaunay), as well as the American boxer Sugar Ray Robinson.

My father had a love-hate relationship with the clarinetists of his generation, and it was sometimes reciprocal. He didn't care much for Mezz Mezzrow because he believed, for good reason, that music was not his strongest card. One night when they were billed together, Mezz had asked my father at the end of the concert: "What did you think of my playing this evening?" My father answered sarcastically: "You can't reproach a man when he has done his best."

He had much more esteem for Albert Nicholas whom he considered an excellent clarinetist, but they had a falling out over *Les Oignons*. Nicholas had been the first to record this old Creole ritornello whose origins were lost in time. He recorded it under the title *The Onions* in 1947. In 1949, for his first session at Vogue, my father used it and added two new themes of his own, thereby creating an original piece, *Les Oignons*. And this one had a huge, unexpected success! This was his first big hit in France which made him a lot of money. Nicholas never got over it. He believed that he deserved part of the royalties since he had recorded it first. This story remained a bone of contention between them until the end. Nicholas also played

LOVE YOU
LOVE YOU
LOVE YOU MADLY
JOYEUX NOEL
BONNE ANNEE
DUKE ELLINGTON

*Wishes Card sent by Duke
Ellington to Daniel and
his mother in 1970.*

at the *Vieux Colombier* when my father was on tour, but he was paid less because he attracted a smaller crowd- a second motive for a dispute. Sometimes after he had played, Elisabeth would take him home and he would not hesitate to criticize my father to her. He told her that Sidney was a skirt chaser who never hesitated to flirt with other women. But he chose the wrong woman to say this to; Elisabeth couldn't have cared less.

I have another story about a well-known name: one night, Elisabeth had a visit at her Parisian home by the American trombone player "Big Chief" Russell Moore, a half-Black, half-Indian giant. My father was touring in the States and Big Chief knew it. Elisabeth offered him a drink out of politeness. They were talking when all of a sudden he threw himself at her and tried his best to kiss her. My stepmother just had time to jump to the side out of the way of her aggressor who weighed at least three hundred pounds. She kicked him out immediately. His defence was that my father didn't hesitate to womanize when he was on the road. When she told me the story, she finished saying, "I never said anything to Sidney because he would have killed him!" I guess there was no deep sense of loyalty among musicians.

The vibraphone player Lionel Hampton was also a friend of my father and they saw each other for the last time in 1956 on a French road trip. He writes: "After a concert in Paris, I

Sidney Bechet, Marcel Blanche, Benny Vasseur, Lionel Hampton, Claude Luter at the Vieux Colombier. *Paris. 1956.*

went down to the *Vieux Colombier* with some of my musicians, Gigi Gryce, Jimmy Cleveland, Clifford Brown, Art Farmer and Quincy Jones. All of these guys were 'modern', smart guys who literally juggled with their instruments. They all played really fast, like Cleveland, for example, or Clifford Brown who were 'racehorse soloists'! And there they were, mouth open, amazed and moved to hear Bechet's music. They were so moved that Quincy Jones began to cry when he listened to Sidney…yes, really! It was a big revelation for my young guys to hear him. They had never seen anything like it or heard music played with such sincerity. Yes, Sidney had so impressed us that we cried… so that night with an audience impatient to meet Bechet I sat at the drums for three or four numbers. My style was based on what two people had invented, those two pillars of jazz: Louis Armstrong and Sidney Bechet. They're my roots. They are the ones who inspire me… I consider these two artists to be the foundation of jazz as well as the two biggest names.[50]"

Jazz critics and the public have both given credence to this assertion. For my part, I tend to agree, but the communication between the two was always problematic because their status was different. I think there was also a story about skin colour between them. My father was a Creole of mixed race, Armstrong was Black. Both were born in New Orleans, but not in the same neighbourhood. They had both experienced racism among people of colour based on social status and ethnic origin. My father was born in 1897 and Louis in 1901, and those four years were of capital importance, given the speed at which jazz evolved. When jazz started to take off in America, my father, who had itchy feet, had left for Europe. While his contemporaries were recording stacks of records, he was absent from the New York scene. All of this gave them different roles within the history of jazz.

During this time, America had lifted a New Orleans man to the forefront: Louis Armstrong, and there was no room for two. He had become a huge star on stage as early as 1929 and was producing shows on Broadway. He was also more of a singer and entertainer than my father. This fact caused my father some resentment, especially since being the elder, he was the stronger musically at an earlier age. When Ansermet was enthusing about him in 1919, Armstrong was just an eighteen-year-old kid, albeit a very promising one. When they recorded together for the first time in 1924, my father had a more mature quality, even if their duo sounded fabulous. The difference between the

50. *Ibid.*, pp. 185-186.

Sidney coming up from the club at the Vieux Colombier. *Paris. 1955.*

two was also a question of instrument: the trumpet was from the start the king of instruments, and used by the legendary Buddy Bolden, whereas my father did his utmost to bring out the best in himself using the soprano saxophone, a somewhat mongrel instrument which not in common use. Louis had a conciliatory character and was less suspicious of nightclub owners and other managers, whereas my father, with his Creole pride, played the part of a complete rebel. Armstrong, then, became the "King of Jazz" for all of his qualities and for his revolutionary interpretation of the trumpet. It's often said that he created the status of a soloist jazzman. In my opinion, my father started the trend just a bit earlier, but again, it was on a non-leading instrument, the clarinet.

I have also read that Louis had invented swing, but I find this unfair to his mentor, King Oliver. Papa was adamant on this: in *Treat it Gentle*, he tells the story of his friend, the Creole cornet player Manuel Perez, who played in the brass bands of New Orleans in two different ways: in a normal march for parades, or as swing to get people dancing. Armstrong and Bechet had parallel careers that did not intertwine. Still, they did see each other in 1940 to record some albums that reflected all the beauty of this music. They were the two biggest interpreters, they spoke the same language, and their two sounds created a delightful alchemy. Paradoxically, my father found that these albums were not particularly successful because there wasn't any soul to them. They played one last time together in 1945, in New Orleans at the big Municipal Auditorium, and this was my father's last visit to his home town. Listening to the recording of this, Armstrong is constantly in the foreground and my father only plays back-up. They were most probably told to play it that way.

Nevertheless, my father was also a soloist, as one of his New Orleans compatriots, the guitarist Dr. Edmond Souchon, testifies: "I remember that Sidney did this concert with a badly cut up shoe. His foot was hurting and since he was wearing white socks, the hole stood out like the headlamp of a Baltimore &Ohio locomotive! But without a doubt, I had never heard anything so beautifully played. His game was consistently marvellous, notably his construction, starting from a simple phrase and developing a chorus that became more and more complex in an ambiance that became more exciting and torrid.[51]"

There had been a failed attempt in 1947 to have Sidney Bechet and Louis Armstrong play together again. Louis' manager, Joe Glaser, had taken care of it. The date was chosen for a concert at the Town Hall in New York. Everybody had signed up for it and the public was all excited. But my father stood everybody up and didn't show. Bob Wilber was backstage and

51. Quote by Charles Delaunay, 1969.

Sidney and Danny Kaye.
New York, 1953.

he was asked to replace him when it was time for the show to begin, but he didn't feel ready to play with such major performers as Louis and Jack Teagarden. When my father was asked why he had defected, he said that he had fainted in the metro on his way there, and that he had taken awhile to regain his spirits. Glaser held a grudge against him for this. It was reciprocal, and I believe my father had satisfied a personal vendetta that day. When Bechet moved to France, he was finally able to rival Armstrong's notoriety. This is how his popularity on the international scene rose spectacularly. Sidney and Louis met one last time in Paris at the Olympia in 1955 when the latter was touring France. There is a photo that immortalizes this face to face and it shows them as relatively happy to have this meeting. The funniest thing about it is that Armstrong had just done a jam session on my father's turf at the *Vieux Colombier* with Claude Luter's orchestra while Bechet was absent. It's remarkable how promoters and agents regularly tried to bring these two giants together. They often made money out of it, but it is regrettable on an artistic level. The truth is that

New York, 1953.

neither of them really wanted to do it. In 1957 they tried to make them play together at the festival in Newport. The American agent Willis Connover had dreamed of bringing together the two New Orleans style giants one last time. 4ᵗʰ July was also Armstrong's fifty-seventh birthday. In agreement with Vogue, my father declined the proposition. Funnily enough, at that time no one knew Louis' correct birth date. It was, in fact, August 4, 1901. When my father died in 1959, journalists interviewed Louis who said: "My man Bechet, the biggest of them all! May God rest his soul." He added that the sound of his soprano was like a pot of golden honey.

In the sixties, Duke Ellington had reiterated his admiration for my father during an interview. It is an important testimony when you consider that Duke had met all the musicians in the history of jazz, up to John Coltrane with whom he recorded: "Of all the musicians I have known, Bechet was the one who personified jazz the most completely. In his way of playing, he represented everything that is beautiful in it. His entire life he played everything in a completely original way. If he played a chorus of *Clap Hands, Here Comes Charlie*, it was like no other interpretation of the same piece; you had the impression you were listening to an original composition by

Bechet. Nobody knew how to play like this great man. Bechet had his own ideas, and no other musician has ever found Bechet's unique perspective. Nobody has managed, musically speaking, to have the same results. There have, of course, been other great musicians. Louis was a great trumpet player and others excelled on other instruments (we shouldn't ever really compare artists!), but Bechet was unique. I sincerely believe it. He represents a unique phenomenon in the world of jazz, a phenomenon which defies all comparison. When we talk about Bechet, we cannot talk about anybody else. Hodges played soprano too, but he was Bechet's student. Among them all, he is the one who best learnt the lesson. When Hodges played the soprano, he had pretty much the same perspective as Bechet. But Bechet was equally unique on the clarinet. Nobody could play the clarinet like he could. Nobody has ever made wood sing so completely.[52] »

Through the decades, there have been a lack so many concerts in memory of my father. The first important homage in his name goes back to 1960 at the very first festival in Antibes Juan-les-Pins. He had left his mark on this place after having played at the *Vieux Colombier* Club (later named The Village) from 1950 to 1958. The festival started off with a gigantic parade to inaugurate a bust of my father in the Juan-les-Pins pinewoods. This bust played a very big role over the decades as a memorial to American jazz in Europe. This is where for the past fifty years jazzmen from all over the world, from the most amateur traditional musician to the biggest American stars, continue to come and gather before this statue to honour a hero.

52. *Jazz Journal*, December 1965.

Over the years, television shows, and especially those of Jean-Christophe Averty, have not forgotten to honour my father's legacy, reflected through his followers. In 1969 he put on a double "Sidney Bechet Show" in prime time. Memories of my father were still vivid in the minds of variety artists. Les Compagnons de la chanson sang *Le Temps des étudiants* with an allusion to Bechet and Luter; Pierre Perret sang *Vieux Sidney* (Old Sidney) to the tune of *Les Oignons*; Guy Marchand sang *Blues dans le blues* and Les Charlots did a humorous version of *A Moi de payer*, the only waltz my father had composed. While Rinaldi sang the lyrics, the choir of *Les Charlots* punched out repeatedly: "TVA, TVA!" (VAT! Value added tax!) with an irresistibly comic effect. Bechet appeared one last time in 1980 in the lyrics of a song by Pierre Bachelet.

Paradoxically, while he was progressively disappearing from French variety shows, he was being picked up in the sixties by Black American musicians of free jazz: John Coltrane, Albert Ayler and Archie Shepp. Being strongly politicized and searching

Bust of Sidney.
New Orleans. 1997.

for their roots, they cite him as the man who made music for celebration and for liberation. Finally, in one of the last suites which he composed in 1970, the *New Orleans Suite*, Duke Ellington paid him a strong homage when he composed *A Portrait of Sidney Bechet*. Johnny Hodges would have been the perfect musician to play this, but he died of a heart attack at the dentist's and never got to hear it. So it was the saxophone player Paul Gonsalves who did an excellent job with it. Without being directly influenced by him, the great conductor and Black pianist Count Basie had also listened to Bechet. In the programme for his "From Spirituals to Swing" concerts in 1938 in New York, he had declared, "Even if he lived to be 150 years old, he would still be modern!" My father had a unique and remarkable position in that he was able to please both the intellectuals and the general public at different times.

Big international festivals began to take place as early as 1974, , and there has always been a place devoted to the dearly departed greats in them. During a homage to my father in Nice, in 1979, his agent, Charles Delaunay was asked by the journalist Roland Hippenmeyer, "and if Bechet were here tonight what would that be like?"Delaunay answered:"Oh, he would have played them under the table! Oh yeah! Even if he were 80 years old. Because he was a force of nature! Sidney Bechet was a phenomenon and he could blow away his audience. I mean, he blew everyone outta the park! As soon as he stepped on stage, you saw this man, small but very strong. He was a ball of muscles, and when he played, he exploded! I'm sure if Bechet were here, he'd play all those wannabes that come to these festivals under the table- all of 'em![53]" This is a testimony I still enjoy today.

53. Jean-Roland Hippenmeyer, *Sidney Bechet*, p. 185.

Moustache

Among the names that have been close to my father, I really enjoy talking about Moustache who was a drummer in Claude Luter's orchestra. After having directed his own band, he opened a restaurant (he had a superb place on Avenue Duquesne), and he was also an actor (he played Sergeant Garcia in the film *Zorro* with Alain Delon). He was a good man, and generous, as well as a very good businessman. I met him one day by pure chance. I was behind the wheel of my car in a traffic jam in Saint-Cloud when all of a sudden I recognized him in the car right next to me. I moved up alongside the driver, rolled down my window and said in a cheeky way, "Ahhh, it wasn't bad- your drum work on the albums you did with my father!"Moustache stared at me, annoyed and answered, "And who was your father?" I answered back, "Sidney Bechet!"What a shock it was for him! He told me, "Pull over now! I gotta talk to you !" He stopped the traffic and we both pulled over to the side. He was so moved to see me, saying how he

Alhambra Theatre, *1952 : Sidney Bechet, Aimé Barelli and Moustache.*

had known me when I was a little boy. He asked me to come and see him one night at the Bilboquet where he was managing a musical programme (he would later be responsible for the Patio at the Méridien); "You must come and play, son!"he told me, he was so excited. He also told me, "Those years I spent playing with your father were among the best in all my life. I owe everything good that has happened to me to him." After that, every time I saw him, he always had to tell me his memories and anecdotes.

Moustache was the only musician at that time who kind and who showed me real consideration. When I went to see him at the Méridien, he introduced me to everyone. In the seventies he directed an orchestra called Les Petits Français with whom he recorded hits by Georges Brassens, with Brassens himself on the guitar. I remember he would complain about the ingratitude of musicians who complained about life despite having a gig every night for 500 francs. One time I came to one of their presentations. They were doing a show in which each musician wore a different costume illustrating their character in typical French garb: Irakly was dressed as a postman, Zanini was a guard, Michel Attenous was a Foreign Legionnaire, , when suddenly Moustache came out dressed up as a chef, complete with his chef's hat and cooking utensils, and sat down at the drums. The band often faced the total lack of interest common in hotel ballrooms. But that night, Moustache had decided to shake up the complacent, blasé audience. At the end of a particularly dynamic piece, he left his drums and ran up to the microphone to yell out: "Applaud, you bunch of pigeons!" Abruptly taken out of their torpor, the people stopped their conversations and frantically applauded as one. They thought that

Sidney Bechet, Eddie Bernard. 1949.

this was part of the show. It was very funny. Only Moustache could have Bust of Sidney. New Orleans. 1997. done that. He was already like that when he was with my father, and that's why Sidney loved him. He was the live wire of the orchestra. He came with his natural disposition and colourful personality and he could do what he wanted. One thing we had in common was that we both owned a Volvo and we went to the same garage in Marly-le-Roi. It pained me to learn he had been killed in a car accident. I miss him a lot.

Moustache often told me that my father was a hard man. When he wanted to learn something to do with music, you had to understand him very quickly. He was ready to explain to musicians what he expected of them, but they had to pick it up fast. He was very demanding with his music. He had crossed the Atlantic to show the way and expected people to follow him. Later, Moustache came to see me in Garches. He wanted to pass on an important message: "Don't listen to what the assholes say about your father. Leave them to their bitter words." He once told me a story about drugs: "One day the piano player Eddie Bernard who played with your father in André Réwéliotty's band had procured a big amount of cocaine with the firm intention of using it. It was his first time, but he wanted to come across as hip and impress your father. So your father let him show off his stuff and then whispered in his ear, 'Wait for me in the toilet and I'll show you how we do it back home.' Eddie Bernard was happy that he was going to be initiated by someone who he thought had experience. That's when Sidney told him, 'Give me all you got. I need it all if you want to do this.' The pianist obeyed. Suddenly your father took all of the bags of powder and threw them in the toilet and flushed them down. Stunned, Eddie Bernard didn't have the time to react. He was expecting anything but that! Then your father tore into him and called him all sorts of names nine times to hell and warned him never to do that again. He said drugs were the worst thing that could happen to a musician and that it wasn't going to make him play any better. Poor Eddie Bernard didn't know what to do. He came over to me to complain, saying, 'Look what Sidney did to me!' He had to have spent a fortune for all that powder. But hey, we had the same opinion on that."

My father hated drugs and the people who used them. He had seen so many musicians in the USA waste their lives because of it. He told my mother that when he was in New York he had tried marijuana once and it had hit him so hard he couldn't even cross the street. This reminds me of another testimony: in 1949

Sidney with his merlin falco. Juan-les-Pins. 1951.

when he was on tour in Scandinavia, he shared a room with the great saxophone player Stan Getz. They were playing the same concert. Getz was smoking marijuana with his musicians and the smell was bothering my father, so he opened a window which bothered the boppers because it was freezing cold outside. He stormed against those 'bebop boys' as he called them, and the organizer ended up having to find separate lodgings for them. But these are incidents without consequence. I know from Bob Wilber that Stan Getz had a lot of esteem for my father. I think I have inherited the same aversion for narcotics. I was lucky not to have succumbed to that plague. I must have sufficient inner strength or natural euphoria to protect me. And yet, I have been the witness to its destructiveness…! It is so easy to get overwhelmed by events and have habit replace pleasure.

Every summer, papa would play for three months in Antibes Juan-les-Pins. He was a permanent at the *Vieux Colombier* Club which was connected to the one in Paris. Moustache was there with Luter when my father experienced something that seemed trivial at the time. He had received a small falcon as a gift. It had been trained to hunt. Actually, it was a merlin. He loved it. It perched on his shoulder with a golden chain tying its foot to its master's wrist. Sometimes, he would lengthen the chain with a kind of lead to give it more freedom and let it fly a bit more. One night, in the big hall of the *Vieux Colombier*, the bebop dancer Claude Mocquery got tangled up in the chain and broke it. Suddenly free, the merlin flew like a bullet outside and went up into the sky and landed at the top of a huge pine tree. Sidney went wild. He tried to call it down with all kinds of bird calls, but nothing could be done. Soon, the whole town heard what had happened and the townspeople started showing up at the scene of the drama. They even called the firemen who brought a tall ladder and tried to recapture the bird. But the moment a fireman approached the bird, it flew to another branch. The whole merry-go-round lasted until the bird disappeared into the skies over the Cote d'Azur. It was never seen again. Moustache added, "Your father had his worst hangover ever. That night when it was his turn to play with us on the stage in the *Vieux Colombier*, he arrived completely wasted and muttered into the microphone, 'I'm going to. Play in the memory of my bird... Schubert's *Ave Maria*' We were petrified when he started. One note, two notes. There was a squeak and then he fell to the ground, dead drunk. There was a moment of panic and then they carried Sidney to his room. Claude Luter finished the show without him."

Bandleaders

When people talk about the bandleaders who worked with my father, the name of Claude Luter comes first to mind. He is the one who played and shared his big hits. My relationship with him has been sporadic and I must admit there has always been a severe communication problem between us. Every time we saw each other, he would tell me stories that I didn't like. I know my father was not a saint, but I didn't like hearing it from him. He has always bothered me and he even frightened me when I was a child.

Claude was one of those humourless people and I have no good memories about him. He had a strange way of greeting someone by pinching their arm, a strange way of communicating- and I've always hated it. Right or wrong, I've always felt he did not have my best interests at heart. I have had, however, a really good contact with his son, Eric. He is a trumpet player and we've played together from time to time. He is a nice man, charming, and a good musician. I have also had the pleasure of having this kind of friendship with Marc Laferrière and Maxim Saury, among others. They are among the loyal people in this profession and are there to help when needed. I may be repeating myself, but jazz is a closed circle and it's not easy to get along with everyone. You sometimes just have to take a step back. It's a small family, a sort of microcosm, and you have to learn to deal with what's there and keep things in perspective, as you have to do elsewhere; and frankly, it's best not to get too upset with certain organizers and managers if you want to continue playing.

Luter always described my father as a womanizer and a jealous one at that who tried to take away their girlfriends. There were quite a few jokes on that subject, which is common among musicians. Of course my father loved playing practical jokes. Luter told me that during one tour, he had bought a bottle of perfume and sprayed all the musicians' coats with it just to make their wives suspicious. It was fun, and I think true, but it never went any further.

My father was not always a "passport to success" in my profession, especially in this type of music. Also, I am a drummer, and drums are not a leading instrument. There is often more of a need for a wind instrument player or a pianist. I came along rather late, and good musicians are more often trained at an earlier age. There are fewer opportunities to replace a drummer, too. This is why I have teamed up with Olivier Franc, and it works quite well. It's also true that I come from another generation and another musical style, so I am in an established order of groups that have been together for awhile. That being said, for more than seventeen years now I have been playing this particular style in parallel with other projects. I like paying homage and playing this music, but I don't find the same verve and lyricism that I can hear in my father's recordings. The dynamics are different and less interesting on a rhythmic level. The tempo is not as quick - things have evolved differently. I find that it is a lively music that should be at a different beat. A more American style, maybe? It is often interpreted in the same way, without creativity, and sometimes in a monotonous way. Improvisation is often absent in the standard pieces that are played, which is a shame because the musicians are often very good but tend to play faithfully "in the style of..." From time to time it is necessary to know how to integrate the piece and replay it with a touch of fancy. This is at the heart of jazz. It's essential to innovate.

André Réwéliotty often came to the house with his friend, Michelle Vian, Boris' ex-wife. He even came after my father

Sidney with André Réwéliotty's band.

died. He was a nice man, very charming, who had it in mind to teach me the clarinet. He had fantasies of teaching Bechet's own son after having learnt it all from my father himself. It was a bit like a return on his investment. I used to have fun and take my father's clarinet and pretend to blow in it, but I wasn't really interested. This instrument has always remained taboo for me. I learnt about Réwéliotty's death in 1962 when I came home after a school skiing trip . I had arrived at the Gare de Lyon and saw my mother there, devastated. She told me, "André died in a car accident. His car hit a bollard on the motorway." I never had the impulse to learn the clarinet or the saxophone and I regret it somewhat today.

Apart from Luter who started in *Lorientais* just after the war, and Réwéliotty, who arrived a bit later, my father also played with other popular bands whose leaders, curiously

Sidney Bechet, Claude Aubert and friend. Geneva. 1954.

enough, played either the clarinet or the soprano-sax. The
two instruments were popular at the time and played by
those seeking a name. As soon as he arrived in Paris in 1949,
papa was accompanied by Pierre Braslavsky who played the
soprano sax. He led a band with René Franc on the clarinet
and performed at the Club Saint-Germain, alternating with
modern jazz. There was Maxim Saury, a clarinetist who
played with my father at the *Caveau de la Huchette,* among
other places. They even did a show together in 1958 for the
BBC that was filmed at the *Caveau* which nobody ever heard
or saw. There was also Michel Attenoux who directed an
excellent band with the pianist André Persiany. He was a
good soprano-saxophonist who didn't back down from
doing a solo when my father told him to go on. And on the
foreign front, there were two good orchestras which were
good enough to hold their own against him. In Switzerland,
there was the soprano saxophonist Claude Aubert accompanied by such people as Pierre Bouru and Henri Chaix,
and in Holland there was the clarinettist Peter Schilperoot

who conducted the Dutch Swing College Band, which is still active today. As well as all these bands, my father also played and recorded with American colleagues passing through. You can find in his recorded works some sweet moments with the percussionist Zutty Singleton, the trumpet players Jonah Jones, Teddy Buckner and Buck Clayton, and the pianists Lil Hardin and Sammy Price. But the albums with Claude Luter and André Réwéliotty are what sold the most because these men directed the bands which recorded his biggest hits.

Unforgettable Encounters

One day when I was about fifteen years old my mother took me to the Salle Pleyel to hear Duke Ellington's band. At the intermission, we went back stage and said hello to the musicians as my mother knew a few of them. Suddenly, I found myself face to face with Johnny Hodges who was completely floored! Without having met me before, he had guessed that I was Sidney Bechet's son because I looked so much like him. So he took my hand and started calling out: "Duke! Duke!" as he looked for him in the wings. He absolutely wanted Ellington to see me. That is how I found myself between these two men excitingly remembering the time when they worked with my father in the twenties and thirties. Finally, Duke wanted to take me back to his dressing room to speak to me privately about my father. That was not only one of the most moving moments in my life, but it was also the moment when I realized exactly how important Sidney Bechet was to the world of jazz. I remember this unique moment in perfect detail. Duke had tears in his eyes and he told me with his throat tight with emotion, "your father was a genius." Then it was Hodges' turn to take me into his dressing room and show me his alto saxophone. He wanted really badly to show me some things, little phrases, rhythmic motifs that papa had taught him and that he was still using. When you think that Johnny Hodges was one of the greatest alto saxophonists of his generation and one of the principal creators of the Ellington sound, someone with whom he had played his entire life, this was nothing if not impressive! Before playing the alto, Hodges had studied the soprano saxophone because my father sent him sometimes to replace him on a gig. He was greatly influenced by him.

I also met Lena Horne when I lived in Los Angeles with Jolie, my first wife. My mother-in-law knew a lot of people and she ran a jazz club in Chicago and she introduced me to Lena Horne who, upon seeing me, said, "Oh! Sidney! It's not possible!" In the thirties she had nicknamed him "Mister Dynamite" when they were together in Noble Sissle's orchestra and he talked a lot about Europe. Lena Horne was a magnificent octoroon, that is someone with one-eighth African ancestry. She had lived through the dark hours of racism in America. When questions concerning her ancestry came up, she would always repeat, "too much White blood has thinned my Black blood, and there's nothing I can do about it." My mother-in-law also introduced me to Milt Jackson and Earl Hines. When Earl saw me, he put his hands together as if in prayer and said, "Ah, Bechet, Bechet!"I also had an equally intense encounter with Dizzy Gillespie through one of the Peters Sisters (the one who lived in Denmark and had then gone back to the States).At this time I was participating in a workshop with the drummer Louie Bellson in a school similar to that of Berklee College of Music. He told me, "Ah, Sidney! One day I was walking in Paris and I was going by a basement entrance. I heard some music coming out and I just dug it!" In 1977, still in Los Angeles, finding myself on Santa Monica Boulevard, I got to go to a big concert with two big bands, Louie Bellson and Buddy Rich. The American who was with me said: "Appreciate this moment 'cause I don't think you're gonna hear this a second time in your lifetime!" At one moment, with Buddy Rich, there was a soprano saxophonist, a big red-headed guy with freckles, who got up and started playing like a crazy man. I saw Buddy Rich watch him with an annoyed look on his face. The sax continued playing, going all over the place, as if this was going to be the last time he would ever play. It was something horrible! I saw the boss wondering when he was going to stop. Of course, Buddy Rich was a musician, a monument to the drums with a strong character, so a person had to pay special attention to him and not do just anything.

One night at New Morning in 1980, I met the great funky pianist Horace Silver. He was in the doorway and I was with my producer Georges Acogny who said to him, "Hello Horace, let me introduce you to Daniel Bechet. You remember Sidney, don't you?" He had known my father in

Bob Wilber and Johnny Hodges, Sidney's students. 1950.

Greenwich Village when he was the same age as I was at that moment. He told me with his voice almost shaking, "Oh! I thought I was seeing your father there and that I owed him some money!" He then told me that I was his spitting image.

I also knew the saxophonist Ben Webster, an old colleague of Duke Ellington, with whom I played a short session. There were other meetings, like the one with Miles Davis thanks to his drummer John Lee. He came to see me at the Mayflower Hotel in New York. I was composing the music for a film for Bob and Harvey Weinstein. He stayed a few minutes and told me he enjoyed seeing me and knowing that I was also into music. He remembered the heyday of Saint-Germain-des-Prés when he came to play at the Pleyel with my father and Charlie Parker. And he came over and shook my hand! It's crazy all the musicians I was able to meet in New York. in the studios, on projects, or even by chance. John McLaughlin, Jaco Pastorius, David Sanborn, the funky rock king of the saxophone with whom I worked in KIO. Well, I always get carried away when I talk about the people I met, and then I realize at what point all this isn't useful in this book, except I enjoy plunging back into these years so rich in memories and emotion.

To finish, I will mention my meeting with the saxophonist Wayne Shorter. I met him in the lounge at the Meridian in 1976-1977. He had asked to meet Sidney Bechet's son. He told me, "It's incredible what your father was able to play on the soprano in such a short time! He created a language on this instrument all of his own! Before him, the soprano sax was nothing but a common bagpipe barely good enough for a marching band. And in such a short period of time he turned it into a lord!" The tenor saxophonist Dexter Gordon was also a very good friend. He would come and eat at the house with Carmen McRae and Max Roach. He was a charmer, a ladies' man. And I must say he was noticeable at 6 foot 3inches". Whenever he came to Selmer's to fix his sax, it turned into a party. He got what he wanted and brought a good spirit to the house.

It's difficult to note all of my encounters, there were so many of them, and it's hard to describe the emotion. These encounters nourished and punctuated my life as a musician, and thanks to them I have had the chance to work with so many different people. They kept me surrounded by friends and encouraged me to compose so many different types of music, because my number one passion has remained composition. So I don't want to give a never-ending list that will only finish by boring most people, but it is thanks to these encounters that I have become who I am. The mother of Jolie, my first wife knew Lucille, Louis Armstrong's last wife. She was a very good businesswoman and after her husband's death she had invested in a fruit business that worked very well for her.

Johnny Griffin's Dutch wife, Myriam, was a close friend of my mother. They would often call each other on the phone. They met each other through Mahen, my father-in-law, who was originally from Sri Lanka .He knew Griffin and Art Taylor well. Johnny Griffin had asked to see my father's instruments. He told us to take regular care for them because an instrument that is not used can dry out and become damaged. He also advised us to go to Selmer's from time to time and have the plugs changed on the soprano. Griffin heard about my father through Coleman Hawkins, the "father" of the tenor saxophone. Then, when he heard him, he was immediately captivated. Griffin died just before there was the first Black president in the White House, and that's a shame. He would have been very happy to have lived that moment because, like all American Black musicians, he was very aware of his community's advancement in America. In the same way, Elisabeth who was German would have been very happy to have been there at the fall of the Berlin Wall. She told me, "One day, my little Daniel, this wall which has caused so much harm to the German nation will no longer exist." But she said this at the end of her life and she was no longer conscious when it finally happened.

Charlie Parker, Sidney Bechet and Kenny Clarke on the plane from New York to Paris May 1949.

Kenny Clarke

*L*ike all parents, my father fantasized about the direction I would take and the profession I would later choose. In any case, he never really wanted me to become a musician like him. He always said that this profession cost too much when you consider what a man brings into it and that it required too much of a personal investment for so little payback. I don't know if I am a musician because of him or thanks to him. I really don't know. In any case, it was not his deepest wish. I believe he wanted me to be a doctor or more likely a big lawyer who would be a legal expert in case of litigation, no matter the profession chosen.

I met a nice man when I was young. His name was Mahen, my mother's boyfriend. They stayed together for seven years. I thought of him as my stepfather. She had known him since 1966. He was the son of the attorney general of Ceylon (Sri Lanka), and we got along well. He was interested in me and early on noticed my interest in music. He wanted me to channel my energies on to playing the drums.

He noticed my attraction to percussion. I never stopped drumming all over the house, and he said one day to my mother: "You must send him to Kenny Clarke's drum school in Paris." My mother did send me but without Mahen it never would have happened. I was 12 or 13 years old and from that time on music and the drums became a part of my life. Another time I had bothered my mother so much to enrol me in a good music school, the Schola Cantorum. I had a horrible school report, especially in spelling, so I could not get in, but I had dreamed so much about this school.

I was aware at this time that an apprentice musician should learn everything possible, in all disciplines, and all of them attracted me. But the drums remained my instrument of choice. Also, it was the instrument created by jazz.. All the musical instruments had existed before this music was born, percussion instruments as well, but it was the combination of all these percussion elements that had produced the drums as we know them. At the beginning they were rudimentary, but they were perfected as time went on, thanks to the great drummers who have marked the history of jazz. Kenny Clarke is among them, and it was he who put into place a training course for the instrument. He partnered with Dante Agostini, a very good percussionist who played at the Moulin-Rouge in Paris. He was a very good teacher. He also wrote the famous method entirely based on the style created by drummers, especially Kenny Clarke. They founded this well-known school and I had the chance to go there and learn from them. They both had such a complete love of this instrument. They worked together on a music theory, which every modern drummer should read: it became the drummers' bible. But they didn't offer just technique. There was also a reflection on how the percussion was played to develop personal musical expression. This a generation of phenomenal young drummers. Agostini loved Kenny, despite some little problems on the administrative level.

There was an evolution in jazz due to drummers like Art Blakey, Philly Joe Jones, Max Roach and so many others who participated in their own way in today's modern approach to music. For these drummers, there was a desire to create a connection between their origins and their particularly modern style of playing. They developed a magnificent jazz that was very rich; this became known as "Fusion." As its name indicates, musicians began to mix music from various origins, especially ethnic ones, wanting to make things move and create an original sound. These musicians were all fantastic people. Then the new technological advances were added to the mix and gave us the forms we know today.

When I first began, during my classes with Kenny Clarke, we concentrated on jazz, but at one point I began listening to Eric Clapton, as well as Ginger Baker, musicians more interested in rock. Kenny didn't make any judgments without listening first. I lent him these records and he showed a real interest because he was open and receptive to all types of music. He had played with my father as early as 1940. He was only 26 at this time, and he was a promising young drummer. He played somewhat like Joe Jones did in Basie's orchestra. My father noticed him when he first played for RCA Victor. He saw the young man's impressive drive. This was well before Kenny invented the new concept used in the bop style of drumming with his friends Dizzy Gillespie and Charlie Parker. After

1967, I saw Kenny every Thursday at Selmer's, on Rue de la Fontaine-au-Roi, where I took my classes. Later, I also went to see him every Sunday at the conservatory in Saint-Germain-en-Laye, the first jazz school in France for all instrumentalists. Musicians from all backgrounds came to Selmer's to work with Kenny. I was always there at 2pm, and one day I came across Max Schwind, who was also there to take some classes. I can still see him with his freckles, very shy and in the corner. He wasn't at all well known. Then he became the drummer for Santana. I also saw the organist Eddy Louiss who also came to take drum lessons. Sometimes some Brazilian percussionists came by. They played really badly, and Kenny would put them right so they could learn from each other, rather like in a master class. I also crossed paths with Christian Vander who founded the group Magma and with all the studio sharks at La Place de Paris. Even classical percussionists came because they knew they had something to learn here, too. I saw timpanists who discussed tertiary and binary time because they wanted to play something other than classical music. Everybody in this small world came to share their experiences with Kenny Clarke as the master of ceremonies.

Now young drummers all have this double culture which was not the case in the sixties and seventies. The most fantastic thing with Kenny was his kindness and caring nature and the fact that he spoke fluent French. He had learnt it very quickly, as soon as he arrived in France in 1948, during Dizzy Gilliespie's big band tour. This was one year before my father made his own big return to France. Kenny had decided to "jump ship" and settle down in Europe because he was so much better treated there. He was part of the John Lewis' Modern Jazz Quartet who were touring the United States and he had talked about it with the saxophonist Johnny Griffin. Once he had installed himself in Europe, though, he reproached himself for his decision to leave and regretted it because he had loved the vibraphonist Milt Jackson, and this new concept of bebop pleased him a lot. It was harmonious and rhythmic, wonderfully melodic and. It influenced so many other musicians, especially in the eighties, in bands like Steps Ahead (with Brecker and Mainieri Peter Erskine).

When I was 19, on Kenny's advice, I went to study percussion at a school in Berne. It was strictly a percussion class. My mother went with me and they thought she was my partner, which perturbed them a bit as they had seen us look at the bedrooms together. The teacher was a good drummer who taught jazz, but in a very scholarly manner. We shared our different techniques with the other students. At the time I had a girlfriend with whom I was very much in love and so I didn't want to spend too much time there. I had a room where I rehearsed every day. One day my teacher called me to say he couldn't keep me. He told me: "Your level is too advanced in relation to the other students and even for me. I don't have anything to teach you." I have to say that I had worked six years with the master Kenny Clarke, learning technique, music theory and, very importantly, the sense of tempo which also needed to be developed, stuff that is not only in books. I stayed just about a month at this school, but it was a good experience. Berne is a very beautiful city with all of its jewelry stores and its arches.

You have to be willing to take risks in music, but you have to work at it. Developing your technique is the key to helping you fall on your feet, and that's true for any instrument. Even with an infallible sense of rhythm you cannot leave out technique. I also worked with Art Taylor when I was 15 or 16 years old. With him, it was bebop all the way, and he taught me the rudiments. It was in the spirit of Art Blakely and the Jazz Messengers. I asked him about the quality of his choruses and one day on the doorstep, he confided to me: "When you go into a solo, you mustn't stumble. It's like taking a beautiful woman home, hoping it'll go a bit further. You mustn't make any mistake in what you're gonna tell her. To do a beautiful solo, you have to be in this exact frame of mind. You must give the best of yourself in a very short period of time."

I still have this image of Kenny, the perfect gentleman. He was always elegantly dressed and he often smoked his pipe. He was the picture of strength and tranquility. Thanks to him, and his ability to bring out the latent talent in a pupil (provided there was a little of it), I had access to all styles of jazz. There were things I discovered on my own, of course, but one thing I learnt from him was jazz-rock which I discovered through his teaching.. Just listening to his way of playing, I was able to develop my own style without being boxed in. His own style was a synthesis of everything that had preceded him. When he played in a band, nothing escaped him. He heard it all and he was constantly ready to find other ways of creating the group's sound. He often said, "To be a good musician, you mustn't be thinking about yourself." The same thing goes for the singers. You have to know how to accompany them, and this is done by listening. A singer never interprets a song in exactly the same way each time. One day she might be sad, and the next day she might give an upbeat version. A day later she may be more detached and you must adapt yourself to her mood. It's as if you are offering her a chair: she needs to feel comfortable. You have to be attentive to the least change in her way of singing. You can't play like a machine. That's why there are often clashes between singers and the accompanying musicians. Listening to each other is important."

The Profession

What I've written above brings me to the subject of La Velle, the singer whom I accompanied for a good while. We did a lot of festivals together. We played at The Hague in Holland, and at Montreux ; we also played at the *Théâtre de la Ville* in Paris and Antibes Juan-les-Pins. She had recruited me through a percussionist who was a mutual friend, Sidney Thiam. I went to see her at *La Chapelle des Lombards* and we rehearsed a bit at my place where I had a piano and some drums. La Velle taught me a lot about how to accompany singers. It was important to concentrate constantly because her interpretations of songs varied considerably from time to time according to her mood. She had a rather difficult character, as is often the case with blues singers. She could be rather moody and quick-tempered, but she was an interesting person with an interesting past. You had to do what she wanted. The time we went to the festival in Antibes, Jean-Christophe Averty filmed us and for the sound track she was inflexible. I ran across Averty several times afterwards, once at Society of Authors, Composers and Editors of Music (SACEM). He was cordial but rather distant because he was such a busy person.

One day when we were playing in Switzerland, they kept offering us white wine all evening. I wasn't drunk, but I don't remember the last set. The cymbals seemed a bit far away; at times they were very small then very big. La Velle saw that I was not in my usual state, but she didn't hold it against me. I was never much of a drinker. I didn't begin to drink a glass or two of wine until I was in my thirties. It's ironic that I discovered the great French wines in Los Angeles. Americans love them. I think La Velle now lives in Switzerland. The last time I saw her, though, she was performing at tea dances at the Méridien Hotel in Paris.

There were times when I lived pretty well, but not at the level people might imagine. I've never bought myself a yacht, for example, but I could have opted for that lifestyle. I have had several beautiful cars including a Rolls Royce. The gossip among the musicians in Paris that there were two Black guys that were driving around in Rolls. They were Memphis Slim and Daniel Bechet. I also bought a Jaguar and a Daimler. That was my wealthy period which lasted a few years. The last Rolls I had was a Silver Shadow 2 Magnolia which I sold back after a year when I had my first tax audit. But I was discreet unlike Memphis Slim! He went to work at the *Caveau de la Huchette* in his Rolls. One time we passed each other on the Rue de Rivoli around three o'clock in the morning. We were cruising down the street, side by side and Memphis said to me: "Hey man, what the fuck you doing here? You think your father would be proud if he saw you now?" We had a good laugh. On another amusing occasion I was going to a week-long gig in Paris with La Velle. It was at the Bilboquet when Bernard Zacharias was the manager. On the last day I had to take down my drums, and, as my usual pick-up was in the shop for an overhaul, I had taken my Rolls. I was parked right outside the club on Rue Saint-Benoît, when suddenly I saw Zacharias in the entrance screaming: 'Who do they think they are! Look at him! Look at what this man rolls in!'Then he saw me, froze, looking at me loading my stuff, and he yelled out at me: "Now I understand that face you made at me. With the couple of bucks I give you, you must have a hard time filling up the tank."

I did my military service in 1974 at the Quartier Gramont in Saint-Germain-en-Laye. I knew the area because I had lived there for two years when I was at the Jesuit school at Saint-Erambert, in my childhood. The barracks were right across the street. After I had gone through basic training at Montlhéry, I was sent to the CEB (*Compagnie d'éclairage de brigade*), a reconnaissance brigade. This brings me to another anecdote: one day I was told to sweep the lieutenant's office, something that didn't happen very often. It was also the day that there were two journalists from TAM, the barracks newspaper. They were in the office asking the officer, "So it seems that you have the son of Sidney Bechet in your team?" I heard them and I started to chuckle. I could see the lieutenant had quickly realized the awkwardness of the situation. His face looked crestfallen as he grabbed the broom from my hands. I must assume that he had not twigged and so I had to do the same chores as any other man. He put on a public smile and said to the journalists: "Yes, we do, and he's right here! Let me introduce you."Meanwhile, I just chuckled to myself.

The following year we had a break-in at our house in Garches when my mom and I were absent. They took my father's Gold Disc that Vogue Records had given him in 1955. It was a real album covered in a thin film of gold applied through a process called electroplating. We never got it back and the thieves only left the sleeve, thereby losing a part of its value. Luckily, they didn't touch my father's musical instruments. Less fortunately, they had taken the furs and jewelry. The evidence would imply that they knew the house. There was a time when I hung out with some rather shifty musicians who, I thought, in hindsight, could have done such a thing. My mother had not thought to put on a sturdy door on the laundry room to stop access to the rest of the house. She did it afterwards, too late. I would have liked it if Sony BMG could have redone the album for the fiftieth anniversary of my father's death.

My Musical Career

My first musical experience was doing music for a film. This gave me a lot on a purely personal level, being asked to do something you know how to do. I was really happy about it, even if the project fell through for lack of funds. I went to the United States in 1975 to live with my first wife, Jolie. I had met her at the Paris VI - Jussieu University when I had done a jazz-rock concert with some friends, one of them being the Senegalese, Georges Acogny. He introduced her to me. She was American and studying French at the Sorbonne as part of her international law studies. I went to go live with her and I stayed in Los Angeles for four years. One night I went to see Diana Ross who was playing the lead role in the musical. *The Wiz*, the African-American version of *The Wizard of Oz*, at the Ahmanson Theatre with Michael Jackson, very young, playing the role of the scarecrow. I had the chance to see it just once.

In 1982 Georges and I decided to work together to create KIO Productions, based in England. He was the guitarist and handled public relations and I was the producer and composer. We complemented each other and had lots of hopes and plans.

Before that, my musical career had been built around being an accompanist and a musical composer for commercials and short films. Like all musicians, I worked a bit in variety and I had done a song for Nicoletta with Touré Kunda on the percussion. The title was *Zokoue Namatanga*. Francis Lalanne wrote the lyrics. It wasn't very successful but I have a happy memory of Nicoletta as a really nice, positive person who had a strong temperament. I was doing very well at the time, with no financial problems. Everything was perfect and these were the best times of my life.

We had a vision. We got into contact with Peter Gabriel through Georges' sister, a beautiful Black woman. She was with the Béjart Ballet in a dance troupe called Moudra. She was responsible for the group and they had asked Peter to do the music. Since we were based in England he wanted to meet us. Peter is such an extraordinarily open and friendly man, unique in his way, and I must say that he has helped a lot of artists get started. We had a "world music" idea using Maasai voices, Gregorian chants and a mixture of hardrock and funk rhythms. Peter thought it was great and told us he was going to try to do something with Charisima. They set up a meeting with us and the idea sold. It came out with Charisima and then Virgin bought the project. When it came time to sign, the manager told us: "Listen, you have a really, really strong title, but the problem is that you're completely unknown. There's a possible opening in New York. They're finishing a film called *Play for Keeps*. That could get your name out there." So we went off to New York and found ourselves completely redoing the music. We were staying at the Mayflower, a luxury hotel where a lot of the American showbiz world went. I saw such people as Robert De Niro, Jack Nicholson and Robert Duval. Those are pleasant memories, but

I do not want to show off. I just consider myself very lucky.

I also met Larry Coryell, an excellent guitarist who was very popular in the seventies. He was often on the cover of contemporary jazz magazines. He started a band called *The Eleventh House*, which played jazz-rock. They were really good. Larry loved Edith Piaf. She represented France in his mind. At the time of Watergate, the scandal that ended with Nixon being booted out of the presidency, he was a simple musician. At one moment he landed a gig to play at the White House. It was the same day the scandal hit the news and journalists were coming out of the woodwork. Larry found himself in the middle of all this media frenzy even though he had nothing to do with the events. His presence there was pure happenstance. But under the fire of the cameras he became a famous musician and it helped his career enormously. Since that day he began receiving all kinds of proposals for work. We had a project together about a little classical piece, *Matador*, hat I had written. He was into Tibetan philosophy and he said that this had helped him to break his bad habits with alcohol and other illicit substances. He took control of his life thanks to that.

After my New York period, I worked on other projects until my return to France, and I fully benefited from this magical period full of enriching experiences. I greatly enjoy these kinds of useful and unexpected encounters which deepen my own personal and cultural universe. Although I am generally outgoing, I don't really push myself forward. I don't look for contacts at whatever the price. If they happen naturally, so much the better. This is not a good thing in this job, though. It's better to be out there, looking, but I tend to be a bit of a homebody.

Another Style

My attraction to the musical world is extremely diverse and varied and I am often looking to innovate. Well before the start of techno, I was already doing my own little mix in the studio. A very long time ago I had started using Revox tape recorders. Later, I had a four track, then an eight track, a twenty-four track. I would add percussions and do sequences that lasted eight minutes and played eight different times. But it wasn't mechanized. I had to keep everything straight and it wasn't easy. There was a tribal side to it, always playing the same rhythm, keeping it all together.

My taste for the underground brought me to play with Laurent Garnier. He came to see me thanks to a mutual friend. He listened to a piece I called *Medusa* and was attracted to its rhythmic originality, so he hired me on the spot. He asked me to accompany him on the percussion and on the drums in his techno band. I worked with him for two years with F Communication taking care of us. Another time I tried to incorporate some of my ideas into their concept, but they found them too rich, too elaborate. I used patterns which they felt were too complicated with the voices and refrains, bits of melody, all too much based on the musicality of the piece whereas techno just demands repetition. You need to get to the essential and that is where the talent of the DJ lies. You could reproach techno for not being very creative musically. It doesn't create patterns. They start from a collection of pre-existing formulas. On stage they use them as they are, or they deform them through electronic manipulation, and that's how it goes. It can be hit-and-miss, but sometimes there are moments of grace. The hardest part is making those moments last. I'm not against techno, seeing as I played it for two years,

161

but I do believe we often take the easy option. I told Laurent and his team that they were not always aware of the amount of preparatory work that had to be done. They often didn't know the why or the how of things. They just chose sounds, rhythms, sometimes entire concepts that had already been invented by people and not by machines. Everything is done. You just have to serve yourself up a mix, plus a little talent of course. I heard some amazing things in the world of fusion in America, but there are also interesting things being done here in Europe. We have incorporated regional folklore such as Basque and Breton, thanks to techno and, thereby brought these old styles more in line with current tastes. Techno has given them a freshness they had lost long ago. Sometimes I feel a bit frustrated that I no longer work with it because I found it very interesting. One of our innovations consisted in playing techno with a complete set of drums. Now everybody does it.

I have no affinity with rap, but I have worked in fields that had nothing to do with each other. At one moment in my life, I found myself playing both New Orleans jazz and techno at the same time. I was constantly straddling a hundred years of musical evolution in Black American music. African percussion is something that is very rich. There is also the influence from the islands, an extraordinary variety of rhythms, all of it swing, but not at all the same. It's like skipping with a rope: there are so many ways of doing it. The important point is that must be good, it must charm the ear and make you want to dance. I met a lot of interesting people in these fields, in particular an extraordinary guitarist with whom I dreamt of starting a band. I tried to do so, but he was completely unmanageable. He had a hard rock sound that touched me to my bones, and I wasn't the only one. As soon as he started playing, people would naturally stop talking and listen. He was not showing, just creating the sound of the melody. As soon as he started, you would say he cutting through the clouds. But the man never arrived on time, and when he did show up, he was often out of it. It was impossible to organize anything with him.

Daniel sitting on the "Lincoln", with his dad

Jacqueline and Sidney

Jacqueline, My Mother

I would like to return for a moment to my childhood and tell you about my mother and the influence she had on my development. As soon as my father became ill, he went for a cure for his lungs to Saint-Honoré-les-Bains. I always went with him but at one point my mother started to keep me away from him. Two days before his death she sent me to my cousins for a week. When I came back I asked for my dad and mama told me he had gone away on a trip. I only heard about his death a month later on the school playground. My schoolmates had heard of it on the television and they told me, "Hey! Your father's dead!" I fought with them about that. I didn't understand. So I went crying to my mother and asked her why she hadn't told me anything. She said she had been caught unprepared… an unpreparedness that shocked me. It's hard to explain what goes on in your head when you're five, but I was hoping it was not true. My mother's tendency to turn away from difficult situations had revealed itself. Two months after my father's death, my mother sent me, without any explanation, to a children's home at La Bourboule on the advice of papa's doctor, Dr Largier. I just wanted to stay with mama and I cried. But there was nothing I could do about it. I thought I was being abandoned for the second time. I gnawed at my toy car, a gift from my father, the whole time I was there. My mother didn't even call me a single time on the phone. I was deeply scarred by the experience. When I returned home, I didn't want to leave her for a second! Then my grandfather came to find me after one long month. I remember that the moment I saw him, I clung to his trouser leg for dear life, for fear he would leave without me. Then my mother stuck me in a Catholic Jesuits boarding school for five years as far away from home as possible. It was my governess, Agnes, a very kind girl, who would come and collect me, rarely my mother. She didn't want to keep me with her because she didn't want me constantly under foot. This way she could live in peace while she squandered the inheritance my father left me.

My father had met my mother in a manicure salon where she worked. One day he had invited her out for a drink - he was a ladies' man after all, and she had accepted without hesitation. One time she admitted to my second wife, Pascale, who was surprised at her inconsistency: "You don't say no when Sidney Bechet invites you!" I admit that at that time he was an impressive man and very well-known. It was the beginning of the star system. I can easily understand her saying yes immediately.. But my father did not suspect that the child he had secretly wanted would come from this encounter and would change his life.

Before returning to my adolescence, I would like to digress

to the year 1978. A friend of my father's in La Chaux-de-Fonds in Switzerland, Bernard Wagnière, the one who was in the lift the time my father received the telegram announcing my birth, had admitted to me during a tour something that surprised me: "Ah! My little Daniel, you were almost a Swiss citizen!" My father had started the paperwork to obtain a Swiss passport in order to reside in that country with Elisabeth and myself. He was very ill and had entertained the hope of living again with Elisabeth. He was a bit disoriented and weakened, but there were still many things he dreamt of doing. My father had discovered that my mother did not have a maternal fibre in her body and that after he had gone I was going to suffer from her self-centeredness. With this in mind, Wagnière had done his best to act as an intermediary with a Swiss judge he knew and he and Elisabeth had tried everything to make it happen. Unfortunately things dragged on and my father was already sick and undergoing treatment. Finally everything was brought to a halt. I also think that Vogue Records must have vetoed the project because they ran the risk of losing the goose that laid the golden eggs.

My father wanted to protect me. He almost succeeded, and it surely would have completely changed my life. Because of this situation, my father had to go between the two homes and that annoyed my mother who wanted to monopolize him. These were delicate and tiring moments for my father. He suffered a lot from this conflict, especially at the age he now was. To this was added the usual pressure that was inherent in his profession: he was overwhelmed with exhaustion. My mother admitted to me later: "Oh no! I was not easy to live with at that time!" Luckily, Elisabeth, who was very kind and understanding, did everything to smooth out the rough edges. She never criticized my mother, and after his death she did everything to stay in contact with me because she loved me. She also did it in memory of my father.

I believe I know the reason why my mother resented me. Before dying, my father had invited a notary to come to put his papers in order. He had wanted the totality of his estate, as well as that of Elisabeth to come to me, including his copyrights. When she had heard this, understanding that she was to be left out, she succeeded in annulling the choice of executor so she could manage my inheritance as she pleased.

When I was very young I had a governess, Agnes, who took the time to accompany me to the Jesuit boarding school. I stayed three years in Saint-Germain-en-Laye at Saint-Erembert, and two years at Septeuil in Tournelles. That is when I began to turn in on myself. I felt abandoned and I missed my mother. I often fought with my schoolmates, especially when they would tell me their parents were coming to take them out. I invented a different world for myself, based on Russia because, that was the biggest country. You know how lonely kids can

Daniel with a friend.

be! I got into trouble a lot so that people would notice me. For example, I would purposely make spelling mistakes. Only history classes interested me. I have an excellent memory, but my head was often elsewhere. Still, I knew how to be very focused when I knew mama was coming to get me. I didn't want to be punished and not be allowed to go out. I had an enormous need for love and attention. I only learned the basic things from the nuns, like how to tie my shoelaces, tell the time on a watch, and a bunch of other little things, things that my mother didn't care about. She had never wanted to have a child, and she often told me so. When she had known that she was pregnant with me, she had told my father: "Either I get an abortion, or I hand him over for adoption!" But my father was completely against that. He told her: "I am going to acknowledge my child!" That's when he bought the house in Garches. After my birth, things did not get any better. My mother was jealous of Elisabeth. As soon as papa wanted to do something, she would emotionally blackmail him. One day he decided he wanted to buy a houseboat on the Seine and use it as a music studio. She was strongly against it and said, "Don't you realize that Daniel could fall in the water? No, I don't want it!" When they didn't agree on something, my mother would leave the house with me for three days. Despite everything, I was very attached to her. I thought she was beautiful and she was the only constant thing in my life. I blindly trusted everything she told me. She could put problems to one side with such disconcerting ease and convince you that she was right- and all this in a light-hearted way.

After awhile, Elisabeth and my mom finally got along. They didn't have much of a choice. It was always Elisabeth who would

Jacqueline, Daniel, and a friend.

take me to visit to the cemetery. My mother never stepped foot there except on the day of the funeral. Clearing the house the day we moved from Garches I found quantities of mail in the cupboards and drawers and in bags, all unopened and forgotten for years. She would receive a letter, put it down somewhere to read later, but then forget about it. The problem was that there were cheques from recording houses, all kinds of requests for licensing contracts, demands for authorization for film soundtracks and other proposals, not to mention overdue payments and other formal demands. I believe that it all bored her and she never realized the consequences of her laziness, or rather of her thoughtlessness. Mama, obviously, did not want to take care of papa's media follow-up. She did not realize that nothing took care of itself and that it was necessary to constantly manage his royalties, supervise his legacy and especially never to think that everything could last forever. I think, with hindsight, that my father's music would have had a stronger future if there had been more involvement in its management. In any case,

Daniel and Jacqueline.

her mismanagement resulted in a heart-breaking financial loss.

I also suffered from her lack interest in my career..I often told her of my ideas and job offers, and each time she would scupper my plans saying, "You don't need to do that. You won't like it. Be careful!"Since I was easily influenced and malleable, I would obey, often regretting it later, yet I still trusted her judgment. It is difficult for me to talk about my father without talking about my mother. They both were an integral part of my upbringing. I do not hold my father up on a pedestal; nor do I wish my mother in hell. Let's just say that it would not be true to talk about my memories without mentioning those things that also saddened or hurt me! I admit never being supported by her. Life teaches us we have to be vigilant, and I learned that the hard way. She must have had a special temperament, to be able to ignore problems. Mama loved to read a lot, especially detective novels. It was a real passion for her, as was the cinema and…. chocolate. Her time was fully occupied. Her motto was to do only what you want, which is a fine if you live on your own!

I don't think that as a child or as a teenager we can be aware how much we are missing, but it remains with us and rears its head when we really don't want it to. Lack of confidence and timidity are two brakes in life. I often regret my mother's lack of ambition for me. When she would reassure me by saying that everything happened in its own time and that I had nothing to worry about, I think she was reassuring herself more than me. She travelled so much she must have lost contact with reality. It's funny for me when I think of my parents with completely different personalities: he was dynamic, passionate and creative; she mother was lazy, with a big sense of humour but also detached and carefree to the extreme! I recognize that sometimes I am expressing this rather brutally. It is difficult to criticize one's parents and I ask myself if in the final analysis this has been good for me or bad. Unconsciously I find something positive in it, but consciously I'm uncomfortable allowing myself to do this. On the other hand, it bothers me when someone else talks to me about them.

I have noticed it is often easier to talk about serious, weighty matters than about funny and trivial impressions. There is something indecent in talking about happiness, whereas pain excites compassion. That is not my objective, but I can't ignore a part of my life which for all that is intimately bound up with the rest of it. My mother was not very affectionate, and there was a wide difference between my father's attentive tenderness and my mother's lack of maternal instinct. He worried about me. She had the tendency to keep her distance. This created in me a lack of direction, assurance and self-confidence - and timidity, which didn't help anything. It was installed in me at a very young age. So I learned to deal with my handicap by making fun of things and keeping a distance. In the end I feel a great emptiness in me, and on the emotional level it's like having an echo chamber at the bottom of my heart. Love is a weapon a shield to help you deal with life. Thanks to my positive disposition, I have moved forward and have even managed to have an understanding with my mother.

I don't know how I've managed to keep a certain amount of integrity. I'm honest, decent, helpful, naïve, a little inclined to vindictiveness and diplomatic - I hate conflicts. In any case, it is preferable to be hated for what you are than loved for what you're not! With the mother I had, I think I could have become a hoodlum or a dangerous psychopath, a misogynist or just a mean, insane guy. I know and I have thought a lot about this. Despite it all, I've managed to avoid that path and have remained somewhat normal. I have often blamed the world for having taken my father from me, and for my late arrival in his life, thus having to hear from the mouths of others about the sometimes questionable aspects of his life story.. It's not easy to hear negative comments, but it happens. It's best to get the facts and face them as they come no matter how difficult. I have sometimes had the feeling that I shouldn't look too hard to know if what my mother said was true or not. I was afraid of learning the truth and when Pascale exposed it the shock wave was enormous. I held it against her for having torn off the veil of illusion in which I clothed my mother, but how much I thanked her for it afterwards! The fall was dizzying and I discovered that besides having made me a timid child, isolated scarred by the lack of affection, by solitude and by the absence of answers to my questions, there were also lies, I have often been attracted to extremes and I also had to deal with being of mixed race. But my mother knew how to console me about my colour. She would tell me that it made me more handsome and that I should be proud of it. I was lucky and had enough of a sense of humour to get out of ambiguous situations when confronting racism. I have within me, deeply engrained, both the good and bad aspects of Black culture, as well as that of White, concerning the expression of anger

There were good things about my mother, however. She helped me to know jazz and cinema, her two passions which are also my own, and I thank her for it. I have also had moments of closeness with her. In the sixties we were in Nice together and she wanted to go to Juan-les-Pins to show me the bust of my father. We had taken a taxi and after driving around in circles the chauffeur said he couldn't find it. The statue had been moved from its original position. After awhile, the driver advised us to get out and continue on foot through the pine forest, telling us that we would end up coming across it, and my mother answered: "It would be nice if my son could at least see his own father's bust!" The taxi driver turned around and looked at me, stunned. Suddenly he became very helpful and quickly found the place.. Another time when I was seventeen years old, I went on a trip to Russia. The organizer who had come with us had all our passports. While putting them away, she spoke to my mother and said, "Wow! You must have been crazy about Bechet to have called your son Daniel Sidney Bechet!" and my mother answered, "Of course I was. After all this is his son."I will let you imagine the woman's reaction.

Elisabeth

It was during his second European tour that my father met Elisabeth Ziegler, when he went to Frankfurt in 1927. The way in which they met is completely magical and merits a digression. Elisabeth was working for a music publisher and she had gone to the gigantic exhibition 'Music in the Life of Peoples' taking place in the Beethoven Hall in Frankfurt. Countries from all over the world were represented and were showing off their specialties, especially in music and cuisine. My father was playing there as a representative of this new American music called jazz. In the midst of all this mayhem, Elisabeth's ears picked up a strange music she had never heard before. She followed the sound up to the stage and saw that this enchanting sound was coming from a Black musician blowing into a soprano saxophone. My father saw the look on her face and he spoke to her in these words: "What! Surprised? You didn't think you could be moved by a Black man?" and Elisabeth answered, "It's the sound that brought me to you!" As she was German, she said that she had felt as if she were in the fairytale of the Pied Piper of Hamlin who rid the town of rats by playing a flute and the rats all followed him. That was the first time she had ever heard jazz and it transformed her life from that moment on. This led to Elisabeth living with my father for four years, from 1927 to 1931. Thanks to him, she had

Elisabeth Ziegler in Grigny.

the chance to travel all over Europe and share with him the life of an itinerant musician.

She told me one day that it was my father who taught her to drink. According to her, she had only drunk milk before meeting him that first time and one night they were sitting at a bar full of glittering coloured bottles. My father supposedly said: "Stop drinking milk all the time! You're embarrassing me!"Stung to the quick, she replied, "Okay! Well then, I will choose that bottle there, and then I'll try that one there!" And in her own words the night was long! She got drunk for the first time in her life and my father probably regretted that he had taught her. Elisabeth told stories about fights and the consequences that followed. Some evenings she did not go with him to work, and in the morning she would wake up to find he had not come home. She knew where to find him. She would go directly to the local police station and find him locked up behind bars because of a fight. Elisabeth told me: "He was a violent man, Sidney. When he went into a bar, he didn't like being stared at, but because he was the only Black man around, and there were very few at the time, it was inevitable! He also dressed in flashy clothes. When he wore a white tuxedo, he stood out! He was dressed like that the day he came to see my mother because he wanted to ask for my hand in marriage. Fate decided differently."

In was in Frankfurt, in 1928, that my father copyrighted his famous *Negro Rhapsody*. Elisabeth had played a part of its creation. She played the piano a little and my father sometimes asked her to sit down and play with him so he could check what he had composed. Sometimes my father had no gigs but that didn't last long: he and Elisabeth would go off looking for something and making contacts. They sometimes found themselves in places where music was not wanted, but my father would find a way to make himself heard. He had his own strategy. He would put his instrument together, discretely, and then start playing ever so softly. In this way he would awaken people's curiosity and then get their full attention. He would, for example, play a folk tune from wherever they were, watching people's reactions. He knew he had power. Then, suddenly, someone would come over to see him, itching with curiosity, wanting to know who he was, and would eventually offer him a contract. This was the reaction he was looking for.

He had a particular technique when he was in town and he wanted to get noticed: in the cafés at the time there were sometimes doors that flapped open, like in American Wild West saloons. He would ask Elisabeth to go inside and keep the two flaps open. Then suddenly my father would come bursting in, soprano sax ready, and he would start a rousing number right then and there. The people inside would be startled at first but then let themselves be won over by the music. The owner would ask him where he was playing and he would tell him, "Here, tonight, if you want me to!" His happy-go-lucky impertinence worked for him because he was able to obtain many offers in this way. His technique was fine-tuned: to get himself heard as much as possible. Of course, there was also the novelty aspect that helped. People had never heard jazz at that time and good musicians were in demand. My father had been in prison in 1929 at Fresnes following a major altercation, and when he got out he was no longer allowed to stay in France. During this time, Elisabeth moved to Nice and worked there as a dental assistant. One morning, very early, my father knocked on the shutters and whistled a little tune that was a sort of personal code between them. They left for Berlin together because they had many good memories there and there were opportunities for work in a place they knew, the Haus Vaterland. Elisabeth and my father split up in 1931 when he returned to the United States.

Elisabeth had a storybook life. During the war she had moved to Algeria. When the German government' ordered her to return to Germany (they needed her because she spoke three languages), Elisabeth married an Algerian citizen in order to stay in the country. She gave him a great deal of money so he would agree to marry her and give her his name. But it was out of the question for Elisabeth that the marriage should be consummated. Therefore, the moment the benediction was given to the newlyweds and the ceremony was over, she ran away. She pretended to go to the toilet where she climbed out of a window, and her husband never saw her again. After that she was able to attend to her affairs with no problem. My father found her in Algiers in the spring of 1951, and when they saw each other again Elisabeth reproached my father for not having kept in contact for twenty years. He told her: "It's just like I went downstairs for a pack of cigarettes and came back upstairs. Nothing's changed." Sidney asked her what had happened to his big suitcase containing his music scores and instruments. She answered: "Your things disappeared forever during the bombing of Berlin."That is where they had left each other in 1931.

After that, my father married her in Antibes in 1951. When the banns were published, Elisabeth received a telegram from her mother in Frankfurt with the following words: "As an artist I have much respect for Sidney Bechet, but for a son-in-law I had hoped something better!" Colonialism and racism were still strong then. People did not think for a second about the incredible things that came out of their mouths, things that would send them to court today. Elisabeth and Sidney did not get married without forethought. They had a deep relationship that lasted more than thirty years. She gave him all of her admiration and deep, abiding passion throughout her life.

One thing I loved about Elisabeth was her personality. She was a very broad-minded soul with whom you could have all sorts of discussions. One time we were joking about male condoms and Elisabeth told me, laughing, "In my time, when I was young in Germany, we called it a '*Pariser*,' a *French letter*."

Here is another story I would like to share. It shows how straight and deeply honest Elisabeth was. My father, through the intermediary of Charles Delaunay, had signed an exclusive contract with Vogue in 1949 to record albums. What is less known is that in 1951, Eddie Barclay, who did not doubt for a moment the big commercial success my father would enjoy, tried to negotiate and buy Vogue's contract for his own advantage. Barclay came by one day at Grigny and Elisabeth received him. Quickly understanding the motive for his visit, she sent him packing! She felt honour bound to Delaunay who had believed in Sidney right from the start. In 1949 Vogue was a small company just starting off. It was thanks to the commercial success of my father that it grew and became a big recording studio in which many artists of all kinds could make their debut. Nevertheless, I sometimes wonder what would have happened for my father if Barclay had taken over his career in France. Fate decided otherwise and I believe that he was very happy with Vogue. He had complete artistic freedom and he was well supported and promoted.

In the same way that my father had owned his own cabaret in New York in the twenties, he and Elisabeth wanted to have their own establishment in Paris. They did so around 1954 but it didn't last more than six months. It was a bistro on Rue du Texel in Montmartre, in a dodgy neighbourhood. Elisabeth took care of the bar and Sidney left a revolver under the counter and kept two enormous dogs, great danes, Yank being one of them, to keep the peace. There was a big dance floor at the back and they tried to play there regularly, but there was a problem with the licence, and especially with the neighbours. It was a really dingy bar of ill repute, surrounded by street thugs and drunkards who would come around and fight. They were forced to stop this adventure which only brought them trouble.

As soon as I had my driver's licence at eighteen, I would go to visit Elisabeth on a regular basis in Grigny. I can still see the road: I would leave Garches, take the Suresnes Bridge, then the motorway. I would go by Orly and through Juvisy and arrive at her place. It was important for me to go see her. We would climb out of the car, my friend Patrick, myself and our girlfriends, and she would greet us with a big hug. She loved being surrounded by young people because was interested in everything. She would watch us to keep up to date with the new generation and the changing society. She was born in 1907 but she was still with it, although she had a strict moral code on what was acceptable and what was not and a total uprightness.

Elisabeth had rather outlandish parents. She adored her father who was a bit of an idealist and a Marxist through and through, whereas her mother (née Lautenschläger) was an admirer of Hitler. She had his portrait in her bedroom over her bed. Elisabeth had been traumatized by her mother who went through a number of lovers, one of whom was a certain General Fontbona who had been a guest at their wedding, and she hid under the conjugal bed while they made love. Elisabeth feared the unexpected return of her father, and the violent reactions that would have ensued.

She had been educated in the German way by this Marxist father who dreamed of a more egalitarian distribution of goods and money. Her father's theory was that the honour of being a doctor, or a lawyer should be enough without the need to be paid exorbitant salaries in comparison with people who had a more modest living. The discussions were passionate among his communist friends, sometimes turning into shouting matches. Her mother would tell them, "You, you are always demanding subsidies from the state, whereas all we want it to be able to eat every day!"Her mother was a humanist. Of course, she worshipped the great man but she knew how to moderate what she said.

I always brought a bottle of champagne with me when visiting Elisabeth and she would take out the pots and pans. She loved making us crepes. Sometimes she told me: " We have to go shopping!"and I would balk at having to walk up Rue Pierre-Brossolette in Grigny. It was a very steep hill and she would tell me, "Ah! Your father loved walking it!"It was true, too. To clear his head and build up his strength he would take long walks around the lakes at Grigny and Ris-Orangis. That's where he would sometimes stop and go fishing - at that time there wasn't as much pollution as there is today. It was a very calm spot and I remember the Grigny clock tower because the house was right across the street.

Elisabeth returned often to the first time she saw me when

Fishing at the Grigny Lakes.

I was a new-born baby. It wasn't easy for her in the beginning because she had seen my birth as my father's treachery to her. At first, she refused to see me. My father brought me over in a baby basket which he put on her doorstep and pretending to leave. When she opened the door, she fell in love with me! She told me later: "When I finally saw your big bright eyes staring up at me, I fell hook, line and sinker for Sidney's son." Much later she adopted me and spoilt me as if I was her own son. She was a sort of grandmother for me because there are after all two generations between us. She was a person of good will who knew how to solve conflicts, a rare quality. I loved her dearly and miss her enormously. She was very dynamic and young at heart, always surrounded by people with whom she loved to party. We were never bored in her company. Although she had had a hard life, Elisabeth was not a victim. She was someone who was strong and grabbed life with both hands.

The house in Grigny adjoined that of the Dalians next

door and Elisabeth was their friend. After having worked as a decorator, Robert Dalian sold his business one day and got involved with the philosophical Freethought movement. He was the secretary and he installed sophisticated equipment in his basement where they printed the Freethought newspaper. He had written and published among other things a book that refuted all the theories based on the Bible. He was an anti-clerical and anti-militarist firebrand. He spent all his energy on this, and consequently his marriage did not survive. Freethought is a movement that still exists. I saw the association has a sign over a big shop on Rue des Fossés-Saint-Jacques in Paris, right in the middle of the Latin Quarter.

In the eighties, Elisabeth no longer lived in her house because the heating system hadbroken down. In a helpful, friendly gesture, Dalian offered her the use of his basement and, as thanks, Elisabeth helped him collect articles and publish them in the movement's newspaper. They stayed a long time together. Then I lost contact with her because I was travelling a lot. I finally found her again when she was hospitalized in Juvisy, and it was a shock seeing her. She had completely let herself go and alcohol had had a devastating effect on her. I found her a room in a retirement home in Les Mureaux, but she never liked it there. She complained of being maltreated. One day in 1986 she ran away from the place and I started a real 'woman hunt' until I found her. After talking to some neighbours - and one couple in particular who lived in a caravan and drank *Pernod* all day long – I discovered she was hanging around with a gypsy and going from place to place. She was really slumming it. In fact, the couple in the caravan had been staying in one place because they had a covetous eye on Elisabeth's house. It had been completely emptied and I decided it was time to sell it. It was in a bad state and hadn't been taken care of in years. I had a hard time getting Elisabeth out of this bad situation and finding her a decent retirement home. Once I tried to have her live with Pascale and me in Garches, but it turned out to be untenable. She needed medical supervision. After a lot of administrative hassles, we finally found the Lelégard retirement home in Saint-Cloud where we went to visit her regularly. That's where she spent her last peaceful days until she died in 1995.

Pascale

I met my second wife in America. At that time I was proud to be working with great American musicians on sound tracks for films, and I bragged about all that to her sister: "I signed with the Americans. I'm at the Mayflower, a super hotel. When I open the window I have a view on Central Park, I have a 200 to 300 dollar expense account every day. I have a limousine with a chauffeur whenever I want him." For the first time I didn't owe anything to my name, but to what was I making of myself. So this friend told me, "You should call my sister." I already knew her, but there wasn't anything between us yet. So I called Pascale and she appreciated it, but we were only really good friends, and it made me happy to speak French again. She was in Wyoming and I started to call her often. In fact, she was at her future husband's house, but I didn't know that, otherwise I would not have been so insistent with my phone calls. I called her every day, sometimes several times because we had a lot of fun talking together. We were two French people in America and we had the same sense of humour. The relationship started like that and we returned to France together since Pascale had broken it off with her American fiancé whom she found boring. I returned home to Garches. We were married, but we didn't have the child she was expecting. I didn't feel ready. I was afraid of not being good enough and not being able to know how to teach him the important things. I love children a lot though having remained a big child myself. I think now I would have made a good father…!

I admit to having lived a very intense relationship with Pascale. We always remained very close, even if our paths separated. The beginning was dramatic because of a new wake-up call from the income tax people. We took care of things on a day-to-day basis, and it allowed me to turn to my father's music, something I didn't dare do for myself. At the beginning I didn't want to touch my father's musical patrimony but then Pascale convinced me to do so and now I don't regret it. I started more by need than by conviction. Now it's the opposite so, finally, everything has fallen into place.

To return to the beginning before my meeting up with Pascale, I would like to mention a strange but pleasing fact which shows that when you want to believe in things, they happen. We were in New York with Georges Accogny on Columbus Avenue. We were walking along quietly, full of dreams, a smile on our lips when I suddenly slowed down before a young man on the pavement. He was French and was dealing out a set of Marseille Tarot cards. Personally, I feel doubtful about them but I like to keep an open mind. So I let myself be tempted. He told me I was going to meet a woman with whom I would live a long and beautiful love story and that she would help me to burnish my family name, as well as a heritage that had been left to flounder and that she would guide me. The next day, I went to fetch Pascale from the airport and we spent twenty years together.

Everything he said came to pass. When I met Pascale, I started to be aware of who I was, of my value, as well as what I was missing and my weaknesses. With much courage she helped me to live with my ghosts. It's crazy how the dearly departed can take up so much space! The problem was with the wrong or bad place they occupied. My father, for example, was a taboo subject because I didn't know how to deal with it. Even his death had been taken from me when my mother did not deem it necessary to inform me. These are often problems that the children of celebrities face. Their parents belong to the public....and we are only alink, a likeness, an offspring... people often expect certain things from us. When we remain anonymous, our mistakes do not show up as irreversible failures. In our case things get blown out of proportion and we feel overexposed.

Pascale and Daniel

Traditional Jazz in France

I made my first contact with traditional jazz at the Hot Club on Rue Pavée in Paris. It was rather "baroque". I never thought I would one day play a sousaphone. I didn't even know the instrument. I also gave drum lessons at this time, which was both hard and fun. When I began playing all of my father's pieces, I knew them all because I had heard them so often. But knowing a piece and playing it are two different things! I had to learn the rules and codes that govern this music just like anybody else. I must say that at first I knew my father's music as played by his disciples better than the original versions which he had done himself. That helped me to start off calmly. The overall result was pretty much positive.

In my previous projects, besides doing music, I was also responsible for the production, meeting people and selling the product. When I was in New York, I had constantly to have the reflexes of a salesman because for them 'time is money.' New Orleans was the exact opposite. I didn't have all this additional pressure to deal with, and the contrast couldn't have been more obvious. Instead of calling them, they called me and I would come and play. I didn't have to take care of anything, and that was much more relaxing, believe me! On stage, the bandleader had to pay special attention to getting the programme together, choosing the right numbers and play them at the correct tempo. Otherwise the public came to hear what they already knew, and everything went pretty smoothly. Of course at the end of the concerts, numbers of people would come to see me and tell me how much they had loved my father and how much I resembled him. It's nice to hear this once or twice, but after awhile it got to be too much. But I always had great respect for the public who had idolized my father. That being said, I would also like to mention certain judgments that I perceived little by little from some musicians and amateur players. I met people who specialized in traditional jazz who had not liked Bechet because they could not stand the soprano sax.. Others told me: "Your father was a genius, but it's such a shame that he didn't stay with the clarinet!" I heard someone else say that he bleated like a goat on his soprano and that his vibrato was vulgar. I also heard others wax excitedly about my father's American albums, the "New Orleans Feetwarmers," as they would say importantly - and they wanted to throw all his French vinyl records in the trash can! It's amazing! I also remarked that it was always the mediocre musicians who gave the most severe criticisms. In my opinion, my father made great albums in France. One title offers a perfect example: his rendition of September Song at Pleyel with Luter's orchestra. It is a masterpiece that stands on its own.

A little bit later, I met Olivier Franc through my friend

Fabrice Zammarchi. Olivier was the great specialist of my father's musical career in France. He is about my age and he did not know my father, but his father, René, at the age of nineteen, was one of the very first musicians to accompany Sidney to France. Olivier is the one soprano saxophonist who is capable of imitating my father's style and plays his music the most faithfully of them all. Fabrice and Olivier paid me a visit one day so I could show him my father's soprano sax. I think I made them happy that day. For them it was like the Holy Sacrament. I then started to tour a lot with Olivier after which he asked me to play in his band. We did a lot of concerts, played in jazz clubs like the Huchette and the Slow Club. We played on world cruises and at festivals, in particular the one at Antibes Juan-les-Pins where they performed frequent tributes to my father. We were always well received. Before playing this music, I did not realize how much it was still present in the hearts of the French public. Though this public of the past generation is ageing inexorably, the baton has been passed and there are a whole lot of new fans. In reality, *Petite fleur*, *Les Oignons* and *Dans les rues d'Antibes* all now belong to the cultural heritage of France These pieces exist in the collective memory and the younger generation reacts favorably to them in the same way that they still enjoy the accordion or the songs of Edith Piaf., Nevertheless, what bothers me with musicians who strictly play nothing but New Orleans jazz is their limited outlook and lack of openness. They only repeat the form and not the soul behind it. This gives a stagnant quality to it, but the public enjoys hearing what they already know. They rediscover the sound and the beat which are familiar to them, and we play on their nostalgia. When I play like that I always have the impression of keeping digging the same hole, like a farm worker, but I find pleasure in it nonetheless. I feel like a museum curator, and that is not something my father would have wanted: his wish was. to make his own music live in the present and to stay in the forefront. The way my father played *Sweet Georgia Brown* in the film version with Sammy Price unchain those musical bars and I defy anyone to be able to play that solo exactly as he did.

I also played with Georges Arvanitas during this time. He and his trio were the usual accompaniers of all the big American musicians that came through Paris. He told me: "Daniel, you have what it takes to hang in there!" He wasn't that much of a talker and he didn't need to tell me anything. But I find that it is still his friend Moustache who has best defined the essence of this music and he declared: "Traditional jazz is the best Esperanto in the world, because the saga, the oral and auditory tradition of New Orleans jazz or Dixieland enables a German on the piano, a Swede on the bass, a Frenchman on the clarinet, a Russian on the trumpet, an Australian on the trombone and a Romanian on the drums play *Muskrat Ramble* or *Royal Garden Blues*. These guys who are seeing each other for the first time in their lives, coming from the four corners of the earth, with different religions, languages and ways of living, can play, do breaks, counterpoints, modulations, without sheet music, without anything, just their love of this music, and they will create the same jazz as the one invented around 1920 on the streets of New Orleans[54]."

After much thought, I think I have found a reason for the difficulties in style that I come across when I am in a traditional jazz band. It's found in my father's recorded work.

54. *Moustache, Tambour battant*, Paris, Julliard, 1975, p. 106.

Focusing on his attentive listening, I can see that there was a constant evolution that followed the drummers he used. In his very first session in 1923, there wasn't any drummer: the banjo and the piano marked time. But my father was freeing himself from these limitations with his new concept that was ahead of his time. Ten years later, the rhythms had evolved. Chick Webb played at the golden evenings at the Apollo in New York, and what a sight it was to see how the people were dancing to his big band- it was extraordinary! It was swing in its purest state and that's where, in 1932, my father recorded six exciting numbers with his New Orleans Feetwarmers. He then played with Noble Sissle's big band which also showed a remarkable rhythmic flexibility. In 1938, he even found himself playing Carnegie Hall with Count Basie's drummer, Joe Jones, who fitted him like a glove! This did not hinder him from also playing with Baby Dodds and Zutty Singleton, the two heroes of New Orleans drums who also evolved toward more supple conceptions. Finally, my father worked with the finest of the fine drummers, the one that everyone bent over backwards to get: Sidney Catlett. He was swing incarnate, with a marvellous suppleness and an impressive drive! I also know that my father groused about Coleman Hawkins who appropriated this drummer because he had the means to pay him top money.

Always on the lookout for talent, my father went immediately for Kenny Clarke when he first heard him, and he took him for a session as early as 1940. Later, at Eddie Condon's club, he even played with Buddy Rich - and it was a catastrophe! I'm telling you all this just to say that papa played with the biggest American drummers who did not care what style was the best. They could go from a quartet to a big band with one password: swing! Of course, I must add that he also played with average American drummers, second rate players. When he arrived in France, the contrast was terrible, something he didn't expect. In the early fifties in France, all the drummers were bad. That's not my opinion; I heard it said by specialists. There were nicknames that floated about in the profession at that time: lead foot, lead arse and so on: we could see where the shoe pinched. But my father patiently explained to French drummers what he wanted from them. Everyone agrees that it is the American musicians, my father being one, who helped them to progress. In his autobiography, Moustache relates how my father would sometimes take his sticks to show him what he wanted. But overall, he played very well and my father loved him a lot, both as a person and a musician. Then Luter hired Marcel Blanche who played swing and was a good drummer.

Guys like André Jourdan and Jacques David did good work on the albums with Réwéliotty. Things improved little by little. When Kenny Clarke set up shop in Paris at that time, he played a big role even before opening his school, but he instructed mostly

Kansas Fields.

modern musicians. At one moment, in Rewéliotty's band, there was a bop drummer called Al Levitt, a student of Kenny's. It was almost magical how the band improved. In the last concerts that were recorded you can see some interesting drummers appear, drummers like J.C. Heard and Kansas Fields who have a very liberated concept, which I think is great. During an interview in the fifties, my father cited Sidney Catlett, Kenny Clarke and Buddy Rich as his favourite drummers. But even more remarkable is the variety of pianists with whom he recorded. When you consider style, it went from Jelly Roll Morton to Martial Solal! There is a whole history of jazz between these two musicians and my father could play easily with them both. Even the notion of style disappeared, and as Bob Wilber confided to me one day: "Sidney Bechet didn't play New Orleans, traditional or Dixieland; he just played 'Sidney Bechet music'!"

Originality and Creativity

To do improvisation, you need imagination; and to have imagination, you need the cultural background. To have a good cultural background, you need to love a lot of different things. You have to have reference points. A person can also start from a single model and slowly build his own identity. This is what Johnny Hodges did in America and he became one of the biggest saxophonists for Duke Ellington. My father gave him lessons when he first started. He absorbed it all and then created his own style and he flew on his own. That's what makes the greatness of Hodges.

After having interviewed musicians who worked with him, I know that my father did not appreciate it when someone was too much 'inspired' by him. To quote Claude Aubert, a Swiss soprano-saxophonist who had collaborated with him: "I have to say that being at his side, holding the same instrument, and believing I could play… one time I let myself go, without intending to. We were doing a number and he gave me a sign to go for it, so I took off on his chorus, basing myself on his album performance… Afterwards he blew me away with a totally original chorus, something superb, all the while staring at me out of the corner of his eye because he liked to show what he was capable of doing! He leaned forward, still staring at me, and did one of his 'tricks', his way of saying: 'Look a bit. Look a bit and see what a person can do!' All that because I had taken *his* chorus, which I often used to play, by the way, and I had listened to his albums once too often[55]!"

When my father played, his sounds came from all sorts of different places. He never started from a pre-existing model, and he continued his whole life enriching his musical repertoire. Luter told me that once when they were out on tour, my father made the whole band go and listen to *fado* one evening at a cabaret. He wanted the musicians to be open to all kinds of music. He felt that there was always something to glean from good musicians and a person had to feed on that. Listening to the influences that show up in his music shows how open his mind was. When my father made his album with Martial Solal, he arrived very respectfully at the session. He really admired his playing and, with Kenny Clarke doing the rhythm, he immediately felt at home. In the album he plays with more restraint than usual. He doesn't take risks and you can feel in him a desire to melt into the group..That day he knew he was doing a very different album from the usual work with André

55. Jean-Roland Hippenmeyer, *Sidney Bechet*, Geneva, Tribune Éditions, 1980, p. 198.

Daniel-Sidney Bechet Quintet at Les Bouffes Parisiens, *Paris,*
2014

Rëwéliotty, even the breathing was different.

Once I found myself in Greece, a country where the clarinet has a long-standing tradition. I had heard a clarinettist on the radio playing a traditional tune. He was playing superb music with such a phenomenal technique and punch that it made me think of my father. He had also visited Greece in the twenties and I think he must have heard something similar. My father was like a sponge with his ear always on the alert, ready to absorb whatever he was hearing, keeping a part to modify and use in a chorus, making it a part of his own expression. These influences continued all his life and that's the reason he never ceased to evolve. That is the principle of jazz itself. It's the same thing with gypsy violinists who have never studied in a conservatory and who play their instruments magnificently.

Olivier Franc has proceeded that way. All he wants to do is

to play in the closest possible way like my dad. He considers his music to be a finished product and he loves practically nothing else. That was his choice, but for awhile now, his son Jean-Baptiste, who is a pianist, has been forcing him to diversify. I played some boogie-woogie with him in Denmark and we were a hit. At one time I toured in a band with the three Francs: René, Olivier and Jean-Baptiste. The grandfather, René, who was a shrewd and educated man with a sense of humour, had played at the beginning of his career with my father. Luter had nicknamed Olivier Franc, "Little Knee" and his father "Big Knee" because they had the same way of shaking their leg while they played. It was a family tic. When I was in Germany with René, there were some Germans who were telling me: "You're not being used to full advantage in this orchestra!" But when I am in Olivier's band, he doesn't hesitate to give me some 4/4 tempo and solosso that I can express myself more fully.

It's difficult to talk about music with Olivier, however. We come from two different worlds. For example, he doesn't like the drums to go beyond their little role of background rhythm. Yet of those inspired by Bechet he was one of the best. Recently, I found two compositions of my dad on a tape which he had not had time to record. This has now been rectified. *I'll Be Proud of You* and *Sweet Louisiana* have entered the repertoire because we went into a studio and gave them life. Olivier did a good job. I am the one who managed to get him known in New York, at the Sidney Bechet Society. They didn't want to hear about him because he was a French musician, and Bob Wilber, who is the eminent authority in America for all that has to do with Bechet, had wanted to block him. I told them that Olivier was the best interpreter of my father's music and when they heard him they agreed. Now they make it a point of honour to invite him. In my opinion, with his musical qualities, Olivier could have gone much farther, but passion is always stronger than reason as we all know.

All jazz musicians, no matter their style, find themselves confronted with the problem of creativity. Either they confront it, or they ignore it but still, it is a question that comes up at some point. Basically, you have a choice of either choosing a master and try to play as much like him as possible, or listening to the maximum number of musicians, no matter which instrument they play and making a mix of whatever you hear. In the latter case, you have more of a chance of coming up with something original. But things are not so simple. For example, someone may become original because he or she is incapable of copying a great master and that's not for want of trying. Or you can also copy the spirit and not the form or vice versa. Originality only asks to be let out, so why rein it in? I can also understand the total satisfaction that a musician might feel when people cannot tell him apart from the master he has chosen. It is more or less a gift for a person to be able to do this in a performance because it is an incredible challenge

Nobody is completely original. Even the greatest musicians owe something to their predecessors. When you listen very attentively to Johnny Hodges, you can sometimes make out in a detour a hint of a phrase from Sidney Bechet, as is the case of Lester Young's song which remained present in the great Charlie Parker's repertoire.

I know my father tried to get close to only one clarinettist when he was making his debut in New Orleans. That was "Big Eye" Louis Nelson, the only one who filled him with joy when he listened and made him want to dance. He was most certainly influenced by this man. For the rest, he drew a little bit from all over, and not only from musicians. For example, in the autobiography of Mezz Mezzrow, *Really The Blues*, my father confided in Mezz that certain effects he obtained with his soprano sax had been inspired by the mooing of cows in the barn! Amazing! He talked about this in relation to his student Bob Wilber who tried his best to sound like him: "The trouble with Bobbie is that he didn't know if he wanted to be a clarinette player of jazz, classical or modern. He could do it all. He had the capacity, and he was excellent. It's very embarrassing and bothersome when you can't find your own personality. He would have loved to play jazz. Bu the played like me, so much so that people would react, 'Say! This kid plays like Bechet. It's as if Bechet were playing.' So it's a bit annoying because you find yourself at a crossroads. A person wants to have his own style, and it's difficult in the United States to have your own style and to be successful as well.[56]" It is clear that my father didn't like it when someone stole his ideas. Wilber evolved after this. He found his own style when he modernized his playing on the clarinet and practising on all the types of saxophones, and my father held him in high esteem and considered him a friend all his life.

Collectors and Fans

The first time I saw my father's death mask was at Elisabeth's. It remained for years on show in her living room at Grigny. My mother had not liked it at the time when they had the mask done. She told me it was not the image she would have

56. Sidney Bechet, *La Musique c'est ma vie*, Paris, La Table Ronde, 1977, pp. 234-235.

wanted to conserve of my father. it was Elisabeth's choice. I respect that choice and I don't blame her. It was her way of taking responsibility. When you see the mask, you can see how much my father suffered in his last moments. Because of this, it is something rather intimate. So, normally, this object should never have found itself for sale. I then saw it at Olivier Franc's where he had placed it on his mantelpiece. He had cut out my father's eyes from a photo and had glued them in the eye sockets of the mask. He also joked about the fact you could still see hairs from his beard stuck in the plaster. And to finish it all, he had dressed the mask up with a pair of dark glasses. It was profoundly destabilizing for me. This was truly the collector syndrome pushed to the extreme. How could anyone be so insensitive?

The first person to have shown his disapproval of the death mask was Claude Luter. He had come to Garches and he found it scandalous that the object had been found in sale room in Rue Drouot. Elisabeth must have given it to someone because at one point her house had been completely emptied. Hard core collectors had come, because besides their sincere love of Bechet, there was money to be made. They began selling his photos and programmes, and sometimes I found that hard to deal with. In fact, it was people close to me who grabbed my father's possessions, and that is what annoyed me the most. Elisabeth started it, and my mother took over. She got rid of all of papa's cameras which he had acquired in the fifties, collector items which were highly prized by amateurs. They had luxurious cases made of mahogany and lined in felt, truly spectacular pieces. I remember that my grandfather had complained to her for having sold such objects because he knew that they should have come to me. I realized one day that it was Léon Cabat, the head of Vogue Records who had them. She had sold them when she didn't even need the money. To convince her to sell them, Cabat had told her: "In any case, if Daniel becomes interested in photography later, he'll buy the latest models."

A few years ago, I sold one of my father's soprano saxophones, the Buescher. At that moment, people thought that I was getting rid of everything that had belonged to him, but that was far from the truth. The sale of the sax was an intense moment, full of emotion and I hesitated about it for quite awhile. But I wanted to do it and I don't regret it, except that I had not foreseen it would land in my circle of friends - in the hands of Olivier! This upsets me on the ethical level. This mythical instrument is being played again and, personally, I don't like that because it loses its historical symbolism in the hands of another person. It is true that I played with the idea of putting it in a museum. My criticism is not specifically directed against Olivier Franc. That is not at all what I was thinking. I don't have an heir, but I did want to open a jazz club and I needed a huge sum of money which I didn't have. That's the reason why I sold the soprano saxophone. One reason why I thought everything would work out was that some time before, I had heard that the Charlie Parker's alto saxophone had been auctioned off in New York by his wife. Its price had reached 345,000 dollars (the price of a studio in New York), and the sax went to an anonymous collector. I did not believe that my father's soprano would have attained this sum because France is not America, but I had decided to give it a try. The Swiss collector Guy Demole got it for 100,000

Euros and I thought he was going to keep it and put it away secretly in his home. The problem is that he then offered the sax to Olivier Franc. Guy Demole greatly admires this man whose fantasy is to identify totally with my father, so I guess one fact explains the other. He immediately started to play the instrument and made a hit commercial in which he said that he was playing Sidney Bechet's sax. For me this object was now no longer sacred. I must say I had so cherished, preserved and gazed at this instrument. It had been a part of my home and I remember how I would put it in its case. To see it now exposed in a commercial gave me a funny feeling. It was demystified and I admit, sometimes, that when I see it lying on stage when we are in a concert I am almost afraid it will disappear. But that's that. It is now in someone else's hands and another story is beginning, even if I think that it will never be as well played as when it was my father's.

I also admit that I am, nevertheless, in a way happy that the sax has remained in the family. Olivier plays in my quintet and I in his from time to time, so papa's spirit accompanies us... almost every time! I've thought about this situation and I am aware that I caused the whole thing. Since the sale, it is as if there have been dark forces acting against me – and it is surely a coincidence. The fiftieth anniversary of my father's death, May 14, 2009, was given little media coverage. It is disappointing but I do not know why the media pays no attention to him today. He still has a faithful following which is renewed every year and to whom he gives joy..Vogue Records and all of its "rescue team," Ferreri, Cabat and Delaunay have profited well from my father's success, and the present managers at Sony have only re-edited a set of two CDs retracing my father's career together with some interviews. There was no big publicity campaign and no television station mentioned it.

New Orleans

Among his many brothers and sisters, born like him in New Orleans, my father only kept contact with his elder brother, Leonard who was a dentist. He played the trombone as an amateur and it was he who gave my father the clarinet, the same one which my father took to make his name when he started playing. Leonard had three children whom my father knew well. The eldest, Emelda Bechet-Garrett, confided in Roland Hippenmeyer:

"My father, Leonard, was older than Sidney. He was born on April 26, 1886, on Easter Day. We had always thought that Easter was something special since it was also his birthday. Papa died on September 17 1952. I, myself, was born to my parents in their house, 1240 St. Bernard Street on January 30, 1925, and Leonard Jr on August 16, 1927. Elmore, the youngest, was born the day before the Feast of Saint Joseph, a big event for all the Italians of New Orleans. He was born on March 19, 1932, around two o'clock in the afternoon and I still remember this day rather clearly. At that time we had moved to the bottom of the street, number 1246, because the 1932 Stock Market Crash had ruined my father, as it did everyone else. So we had lost the splendid twelve- room house and we had to rent one. My father never roseto his old position. However, he had managed to keep a big part of his clientele who came to his dental surgerybecause he had a good reputation. Nevertheless, these kinds of things leave a profound mark on you. No use crying. It doesn't change

a thing.[57]*"*

My contacts with my American family are rather weak. Still, I had a chance to meet a distant cousin, as well as Leonard Jr., who it was that recalled that when my father was angry he dressed completely in black and wore a wide rimmed hat for three days. Leonard Jr. came to see me when I was in Los Angeles. . I can still see him at the bus station, and I immediately knew that it was him when I saw his head of hair- all the Bechets have the same head of hair., At that time he was in having a cure with Alcoholics Anonymous . A very nice man, he had known my father when he was fifteen and had taken soprano saxophone lessons with him. Leonard had first studied with a classical teacher who made him play a steady sound with no vibrato. When my father took him in hand, he told him: "Forget all that you've learned and learn to think for yourself!" He had even recorded an album with the soprano sax on which one can clearly hear my father's influence. Papa had also used him as in his band player on tour but that is what turned him away from the profession. He had so many stories to tell, one being about sandwiches. Over in New Orleans, his mother would prepare such good sandwiches that my father, with his voracious appetite, would eat them all, and that annoyed him. So Leonard thought up a survival plan in which he cut a sandwich in two, including the wrapping to slow him down.

Leonard's young brother, Elmore, I saw for the first time in New Orleans in 1993, during a conference on Bechet organized by the historian and university professor Joe Logsdon. That is where I met my whole family, a whole gaggle of cousins and distant cousins who all came together to see me. They were the

57. Jean-Roland Hippenmeyer, *Sidney Bechet*, p. 177.

descendants of my father's brothers and sisters. Elmore had come with his daughter Gwendolyne, a dizzyingly attractive Creole. We went to the best Creole restaurant in town, and it was torture for me. Smells and sublime scents wafted all over the restaurant, coming from dishes that had been prepared- and I could barely taste them. All evening long I was surrounded by family who lined up to ask me questions and to talk. I couldn't get away for a quarter of an hour, and I must have eaten a total of three pieces of shrimp. I saw all these dishes parade before me and I was not able to touch them. Still, I had an excellent evening. It was a strange experience finding myself in a New Orleans restaurant with forty people all having the same name as myself. And whose existence I was unaware of just days before. New Orleans is one of those American cities where you eat really well because it is at the crossroads of several cultures. They have the best Mexican restaurants in the world -although those of Los Angeles are not bad either. We also went into one of the most renowned restaurants of the city on Bourbon Street, *La Galatoire*. It specializes in French cuisine and it offers, among other thing, *pompanos*, a type of small flat fish from Lake Pontchartrain, which I will never forget.

I returned another time to New Orleans in 1997 to celebrate the centennial of Sidney Bechet. Before that, in April 1996, the Centre for Afro-American Studies and New Literature in English (CETANLA) at the Sorbonne, aided by Harvard University in the USA, had organized an international conference in Paris on "African-American music and dance and Europe." The purpose was to bring to light the formidable creativity that resulted from the confrontation of African-American and European cultures. Among all the personalities mentioned, only one seemed to

Michael White welcomes Fabrice Zammarchi, Leonard Bechet and Daniel Bechet. New Orleans. 1993.

have achieved a career that perfectly illustrated this: the soprano saxophonist Sidney Bechet. A tribute to my father was therefore organized by the Sorbonne on this theme. That day there were successful efforts to go beyond the usual themes. Claude Luter was in charge of illustrating, with his band, the best known aspects of this music. In contrast, Fabrice Zammarchi reinterpreted some of Sidney's themes in his swing-bop style; and even more interestingly, he and his pianist performed the unpublished *Negro Rhapsody*. There was also a re-interpretation of Duke Ellington's *Portrait of Sidney Bechet* by the Swing Limited Corporation, and it ended with a series of concerts with my fusion jazz band Batik. There were some Americans, close to the mayor of New Orleans, Marc Morial, who had come to Paris to invite European musicians and specialists in jazz to come to New Orleans the following year to commemorate the hundredth anniversary of Sidney Bechet's birth.

In May 1997, the city of New Orleans really did things well. The artistic collaboration with Paris continued, and a half a dozen institutions from Canada, Germany, England and the United States joined in the event. The famous Jazz and Heritage Festival created by the impresario George Wein naturally linked up with this commemoration. The organizers also dedicated several parts of the programme to Bechet. Leading their teams were the clarinettists and saxophonists Jim Galloway, Jacques Gauthé, Claude Luter, Michael White, Bob Wilber and Fabrice Zammarchi, as well as the trumpet players John Chilton and Boss Quéraud who all performed in the vast tent at Economy Hall, dedicated to traditional jazz.

There was also a concert done by a team of American all-stars at which Wessel Anderson shone. He is, a multi-talented saxophonist who played in Wynton Marsalis' group and who, for the occasion, played a small soprano saxophone. There was a church service in my father's memory in the presence of George Wein and some of my family which took place at St. Augustine's Church where he was baptized in 1897. It was a moment of great spiritual communion. Another important thing: George Wein had financed a project which he held close to his heart, bringing a copy of the Juan-les-Pins bronze bust be erected permanently in Louis Armstrong Park. The inauguration of this replica was performed by the French Ambassador to the United States, François Bujon de l'Estaing who came especially for the event. Beforehand a gigantic parade had been organized. The procession started at Jackson Square in front of the cathedral. Ten brass bands participated in it. I remember nine of them including the Olympia Band, the Original Liberty Jazz Band, Treme, the Storyville Stompers, Algiers, Pin Stripe, Mumbo Jumbo, Tuxedo and the European Legion.

Before this event, a European visitor to New Orleans might have been surprised not to find some sign of my father's presence in the Vieux Carré, the French Quarter of this town where he was born. It begs the question of how a musician who had found his place in the pantheon of jazz could be practically forgotten in his own country. In the United States, the name of Sidney Bechet is not recognised like the names of Louis Armstrong or Benny Goodman. But his name is renowned in Europe, especially throughout French-speaking countries in Europe, Africa and the West Indies. For example Gabon, Chad and Mali, as well as the island of Saint Vincent in the Caribbean have all issued a postage stamp with his picture which bears witness to his popularity in these regions. Today, we are making him into a myth and imbuing him with a spiritual and dynamic force. Through this celebration in 1997, we brought him symbolically back to his home town. This return is materialized by the delivery of the replica of the statue that honours him in Juan-les-Pins, erected in a special place: the Louis Armstrong Park is in fact the ancient Congo Square where, for centuries, slaves and their descendants were able to preserve the essence and the forms of African culture through music and dance. This musical tradition, nourished by Creole musicians of colour such as Sidney Bechet and Jelly Roll Morton played a major part in the beginnings of jazz.

Charlie Parker, Eddie Barclay and Sidney Bechet. Paris, May, 1949.

THE DREAM OF A FILM

At the end of this long story of which I have been both witness and investigator, I realize that this quest should lead to the making of a film. Rather than a film on Sidney Bechet specifically, it could include in its scope a platform in which everyone could find a particular resonance. It would be a story to make us think about where we come from, to help us understand who we are and become conscious of the importance of our roots, and especially understand the nature of our vocation for those of us who are musicians.

There have been films from time to time which paid tribute to mythical American musicians. In the fifties there was a flowering in the US of films, such as *The Benny Goodman Story*, *The Glenn Miller Story*, *Young Man with a Horn*, *The Man with the Golden Arm* and others. I love all these films. They are like an encyclopedia on American music from which each viewer can take what he wants. Later, other directors knew how to tell the lives of jazzmen in a less Hollywood-type fashion. Clint Eastwood stands alone because he had a strong connection with African American music. He is himself a pianist, and a number of his films have a strong blues ambiance. His *Bird* is without a doubt the closest to this essence, besides being the most successful. The subject was sensitive to treat and he did not fall into the trap that reconstructions often do. In France, Bertrand Tavernier directed *Round Midnight* with Dexter Gordon in a fictional story inspired by the life of the pianist Bud Powell. In this film we are sheltered from the pitfalls of reconstruction, but the storyline is somewhat trivial: a character who takes his idol who is down and out into his home.. The Italian director Pupi Avati made a sensitive and inspiring film entitled *Bix*, based on the life of Bix Beiderbecke. It was made on a low budget and it had a limited success given the rather specialized subject matter.

Back in America, it is Spike Lee, in the same period, who, in my opinion, best succeeded in making a jazz movie with his film *Mo' Better Blues*. He used Denzel Washington in the role of the bop trumpeter, and he is totally credible. You can believe he's really playing. The film also demonstrates a deep understanding of the world in which the musicians evolved and the feelings that animated them. But I think *Ray*, the film by director Taylor Hackford which retraces the life of Ray Charles, takes the gold medal among all these bio-pics of American musicians. The direction is fantastic and the extraordinary talent of Jamie Foxx who incarnates the "Genius" carries the film along from start to finish. He won the Oscar for best actor in 2005 for his role in this film.

Several years ago, in an episode in his Indiana Jones series, Spielberg integrated part of my father's story. Woody Allen has always had a strong attraction to Bechet's music, and he often used it in the sound tracks of his films. I met him in New York thanks to Peter Gabriel when he had just finished shooting *The Purple Rose of Cairo*. He said he was dreaming of doing a film about my father but unfortunately he never had the budget for it. [58]

I have also met one of the people responsible for the writing of the series *Roots*, which was a very successful television series dealing with slavery. I lent him *Treat it Gently*, my father's autobiography. He was so moved after reading it that he told me how sorry he was that he couldn't use it instead of the novel that had been chosen, because the story was so much richer. It is true that there is a constant theme in this story that retraces my father's life, a sort of red thread that begins with the tempo given by Omar and which reaches its peak in his artistic accomplishment. I think that his career, his adventure, as well as the period when he lived could certainly be the basis of a very good movie. For me, this would be the ultimate homage that could be given to him, but I admit not knowing how to make contact with the important people in the closed milieu that is cinema. It is far from simple to get a project into the right hands! This idea of a film exists. It has a watermark and there have been moments of hope, but we still need to find the right person who will have a passion for this adventure and accept the work of transforming it into a universal subject. All the ingredients are there for the story, if it is well presented, to find a favourable echo in the heart of each of us …

---

58. Woody Allen's 2011 film, *Midnight in Paris* features Bechet's *Si Tu Vois Ma Mère*.

EPILOGUE

usic is something serious, profound, and a major art form. It lives first in the mind, then, with rigour and gentleness we play it. No music is easy. Every musician mentioned here in this book knows it. Engraved in us are moments of happiness, and sometimes of sadness. Music wakes us up, transports us. We just have to let ourselves be rocked by it without reflecting. There is no need to be the best musician. We just have to love music to know how to give it to others. The public is not stupid. It doesn't make a mistake even if they do not always see the difference between an average band and one of quality, as long as they are getting something they're looking for. That's what is important. It's when we give the best of ourselves, with emotion, then "anything goes." The magic works naturally. Music, like life, should be handled like a recipe! You have to add quality ingredients in a specific order, with care; and pay attention to them and then mix them together so they can reveal themselves to each other. Then add a bit of seasoning, just enough to tie them together without suffocating them.

I would so much have loved to have been guided by my father, to learn things and especially to learn everything about him! How I wish I could have shared tenderness and experience, learnt from his mouth if what I was doing was good or less good, or simply had his opinion. That is what is called "transmission." I believe I would have felt stronger, and why not, even better. It's crazy how much I miss him. Even today I remain so very conscious of his absence.

I know that he remains in the hearts of millions of people and I am very proud of that. I hope it will continue to be so for a very long time. Now, everything that people can share about my father, objects like albums and photos, no longer upsets me. In fact, I really do not mind because what I have of him is inside me, and nobody can take that away.

The little soprano sax on the « Samson ».

ACKNOWLEDGMENTS

I would like to thank Claude Ribbe through whom I had the pleasure of meeting my publisher;

Pascale Pelletier, my ex-wife and faithful collaborator for the past twenty-five years, for helping me, for her motivation and her participation in this work; Sylvie Mas, a very old friend, for her wonderful collaboration; and, finally, Fabrice Zammarchi, guardian of Sidney Bechet's memory and a close friend.

Pee Wee Russell, Sidney Bechet, Kirk Douglas, Art Hodes in Eddie Condon's Club, New York 1949.

CONTENTS

Foreword 7

   Sidney Bechet - the British Connection 7

Introduction 11

The family 13

   Omar 13

   My Father 16

Sidney Bechet 19

   Early Triumphs 25

   Characteristic Blues 27

   The Song of Songs 30

   Wild Cat Blues 32

   "The Talking Saxophone" 36

   Maple Leaf Rag 44

   Chant in the Night 46

   "School of Music" 49

   Summertime 55

   Les Oignons 61

   Petite Fleur 69

   The Olympia 74

Passport to Paradise 79

Cinema and Musical Comedy 83

France...**91**

La Chanson d'Omar (Omar's Song) and Soleil Africain (African Sun)...91

La Nuit est une sorcière

(The Night is a Witch) 94

The Hill of the Delta..99

My memories and my heritage...............................**103**

Secret garden...103

Montand, Piaf and Mariano..117

Armstrong, Duke, Hampton and others....................................122

Moustache 133

Bandleaders 138

Unforgettable Encounters 143

Meetings and Influences....................................**149**

Kenny Clarke 149

The Profession 155

My Musical Career 158

Another Style 161

Some Women in my Life… **165**

Jacqueline, My Mother 165

Elisabeth...175

Pascale 185

Back to New Orleans Jazz **189**

Traditional Jazz in France..189

Originality and Creativity 195

Collectors and Fans...200

New Orleans 204

The dream of a film...211

Epilogue 215

Acknowledgments..217

Printed and bound in India by Imprint Digital